YOU'RE
gonna get
PEED ON!

Dr. Michael Bugg, (D.V.M)

Before you dive into this book, please note the credentials behind my name. I am not a psychologist. I am not a certified mental health professional. I am not an accountant or lawyer. I am not a financial planner.

I am a veterinarian with more than a decade of clinical experience.

But more importantly, I am Michael. These are my thoughts, experiences, and opinions. While most of the stories and events in this book are true, some names and identifying details have been changed to protect the privacy of the people involved. Also, the dialogues have been retold to capture and express the concepts, feelings, and emotions.

To Riley.

You can be whatever you want to be when you grow up. I hope you choose to be Riley.

Contact information for The Veterinary Project Publishing
www.michaelbugg.com

ISBN: 978-1-7387723-0-8 (paperback)
ISBN: 978-1-7387723-2-2 (ebook)
ISBN: 978-1-7387723-1-5 (hardcover)
ISBN: 978-1-7387723-3-9 (audiobook)

Ordering Information:

Special discounts are available on quantity purchases by corporations, associations, and others. For details, contact www.michaelbugg.com

Contents

Preface   1

Chapter One: **Did I Climb the Wrong Mountain?**   5

Chapter Two: **The Paradox of Perfectionism**   13

Chapter Three: **How to Eat an Elephant**   29

Chapter Four: **Decisions Dictate Your Life**   43

Chapter Five: **Empathy Alchemy**   61

Chapter Six: **The Right Thing Isn't Always Easy**   73

Chapter Seven: **I Am**   85

Chapter Eight: **The Ball Is in Your Court**   95

Chapter Nine: **Curate Your Environment**   107

Chapter Ten: **You Can Do Hard Things**   117

Chapter Eleven: **Let's Pivot**   135

Chapter Twelve: **The Money Mindset Drain**   141

Chapter Thirteen: **New Money Paradigms**   159

Chapter Fourteen: **The ~~Red~~ Green Light**   179

Acknowledgments   183

YOU'RE
gonna get
PEED ON!

How Veterinarians Can Keep Their Dream Job From Becoming a Nightmare While Working Less and Earning More

DR. MICHAEL BUGG, D.V.M.

Preface

FIRST, LET ME just start by saying I love science. I believe the greatest skill being a veterinarian has taught me is the ability to think critically (for myself) and solve problems; it is a very intellectual pursuit. With regard to the care of our patients, I absolutely believe in the scientific process as new diagnostic and treatment procedures are developed.

But this book isn't about that. It's about the care of YOU! One interesting and unexpected development I encountered on my journey away from Miserable Mike (you'll meet him shortly) was just how much of a transformation occurred once I allowed other areas of my body to have a say (and actually listened to them). Things like intuition and "soulset"—pieces of myself that were always there but that I chose to ignore.

There is both an art and a science to being a veterinarian. This book focusses much more on the art.

Of course, where the science is available, I am happy to share it (like the fascinating research surrounding mindfulness, for example), but this book does not read like a research paper and you won't find double-blind peer-reviewed studies for every concept introduced here. Some will require a little courage and a leap of faith.

As I found out, if you always do what you've always done, you'll always get what you've always got. Change requires a different approach. With that in mind, I'd like to invite and even challenge you a little as you work your way through this book:

1. **Get out of your head.** This is not a textbook that you need to study front to back, highlighters at the ready. The real value in this book comes from changing your *context*, not the specific *content*. There will be no pop quiz part way through to make sure you've memorized the Krebs cycle and are worthy to continue. Read to enjoy. The goal is that the concepts that resonate with you should land on some sort of emotional level.

2. **Put the scalpel blade down.** If you wanted, you could dissect every single concept and chapter and point out situations and scenarios where they don't apply. There is a reason this book took me over two years to write. It's because I'm one of you! (I'm looking at you, Chapter 4.) Again, this book is about big, overall concepts that will impact your life. Yes, there are direct tactical pieces that you can implement, but exceptions always exist. I understand that a quick and definite decision may not be the most appropriate in a complex medical situation. Again, art and science.

3. **This book is purebred Bernedoodle that is also part-wolf.** And you have the only copy in existence. You will be reading this book through the filter of all of your past experiences and beliefs, and your colleagues will be doing

the same. That means that every single person will experience this book differently. If you choose to re-read it a year from now, you'll notice that different concepts resonate. It's not that the content will have changed—it's that you will have changed.

4. **I hope we don't agree on everything.** If we do, then I probably haven't written anything very interesting and certainly nothing outside your comfort zone. I also look forward to looking back on this book in 20 years and wondering what the hell I was thinking, because *that is the journey of growth*. We are supposed to refine or outright replace our thoughts and beliefs as we evolve. This is where art and science can actually meet.

My sole intention in sharing this book is to positively impact each and every reader, and, ultimately, the veterinary profession. I am honored and grateful that you have chosen to spend some of your time here.

Chapter One

Did I Climb the Wrong Mountain?

I REMEMBER IT LIKE it was yesterday.

I was fresh out of veterinarian school and on my way to the veterinarian clinic for the first time—but I wasn't feeling how I thought I would. *Aren't I supposed to be excited? What's wrong with me?*

I had put in YEARS of hard work to get to this point, and yet here I was, staring at a looming red traffic light as a sinking feeling started to settle in my stomach. The route to the clinic only had three traffic lights on it, but on that day, they were all red. Time seemed to stretch out into excruciating eternity.

I neared the last red light and slowed to a stop. Looking around, I realized I was alone—the first and only vehicle traveling in my direction. Suddenly, my thoughts took a total grip on my mind, tumbling onto each other. A lump grew in my throat, stealing my breath. As my heart began to pound against my chest, I clutched the steering wheel with a white-knuckled grip.

And then it hit me: *What the hell have I done?*

It Began with Good Intentions

Fifteen years prior, I was awakened by the sound of excited commotion. I rolled over in my bed, glanced out my window at the still-dark sky, and checked my alarm clock: 4:00 a.m.

Despite every bone in my body asking me to stay in bed, exhilaration took over. I rushed out of bed, threw on a coat, and followed the sound of my parents' chatter. Their voices led me outside of my house and into the cold, Saskatchewan night. Across the way, inside the barn, I spotted a dim light and heard the hoarse bellowing of a cow. Still half-asleep, I rubbed my eyes and thought, *it's happening!* I wasn't tired anymore.

I picked up my pace and ran toward the barn, my small feet crunching over the frozen white ground beneath me. Once I neared the barn doors, I was finally able to peer through a crack. Inside, I saw my parents and our local veterinarian, huddled together around a pregnant cow.

Having grown up on a cattle farm, I was used to the typical, scheduled visits from our vet, but this was different. And I wanted to be a part of it.

The door creaked as I opened it, initially startling my parents, but they met my interest with a smile. I walked into the barn just as the vet was firing up his clippers, ready to shave the cow's side. He was homed in on his craft, seeming to me like a god masterfully navigating a tense situation. He didn't notice me, but I was okay with that.

I watched from afar as the rest of the scene unfolded, with everyone gathered around the vet and the cow. With awe, I observed as he worked so symbiotically with a patient that couldn't speak to him. Then, a mother gave birth to her baby.

That was the night I started to consider a future in veterinarian medicine.

Looking back on my childhood, it seems that my career path was almost inevitable. Pets were a staple in our household. You could find me playing with the animals on our farm from the second I stepped off the school bus until my parents forced me to come inside when nighttime came around. For me, this mostly meant my 4-H steers, my dog, and our farm full of 21 barn cats—wow, we had lots of cats!

I couldn't help but be fascinated by animals. I'm sure you can relate.

When I was young, I would spend *hours* trying to get one step closer to a wild steer or attempting to gain the trust of a feral cat by feeding it, just so I could pet it. Given enough time, there wasn't a critter on our farm that I couldn't tame and eventually become friends with—and it's easy to understand why! Few things match the special bond that can form between animals and humans. Pets can provide companionship, give us purpose, and become an important part of one's family—but it goes even further than that. Some days I felt like my animals were the only ones that truly understood me.

As I got older, my interest in a veterinary career grew stronger, especially in the summer of 1995. That was the year my sister got into a serious car accident and suffered major head trauma. It led to permanent disability and an inability to continue her education, so from then onward, my parents focused on her care.

Up until that point, I hadn't put in much effort to get good grades, while Jill was celebrated for her academic achievements. But after Jill's devastating accident, I quickly became an honor roll student and even skipped a grade—from grade 6 to grade 8.

However, there was more happening under the surface of me just wanting to succeed in school. I was stepping into the role Jill used to play in our family and was getting praise for doing so. I really wanted to please everyone, and the more I did, the better I did in school.

All the while, I was growing nearer and nearer to becoming a veterinarian, without ever stopping to consider why I wanted to become one in the first place. But after taking an aptitude test in grade 11 that suggested I become a vet, confirmation bias sealed my fate.

I continued excelling at school for validation on auto-pilot mode until I got into university. After receiving a bounty of encouragement from friends and family at the end of my second year, I decided to look into applying for veterinarian school. When I saw the application fee was only $50, I thought, *What the hell, it's not like I'll actually get in!*

To my surprise, I was admitted.

As I read the acceptance letter, I knew I was supposed to feel elated about my achievement, but for some reason, I didn't. It was only as news of my acceptance spread through the grapevine, and I received overwhelmingly positive feedback that I thought, *I guess I'm going to vet school!* I know my experience may not be a common one or may only somewhat resonate with you, but my path was always heavily influenced by the validation of others.

Everyone Loves a Veterinarian

And that brings us back to that fateful day, staring into the red light.

Had I made a mistake? I was about to spend the next 30–40 years of my life making this exact same drive—maybe not on this same road or to this same clinic—every day of my life. *Is this it?* I thought.

I went back to the beginning. Back to that night in the barn. Back to that acceptance letter.

Because the route to becoming a vet is so defined and specific, I had focused all my energy on getting closer to the end goal and had never stopped to consider what becoming a vet really meant. Clearly, I hadn't given enough thought to the rest of my life.

It was in that moment, staring at that red traffic light for what seemed like forever, that I realized I felt trapped. I had finished the schooling, done all the tests, and pinned a "D.V.M." next to my name—I had done everything I was supposed to do, but I wasn't happy.

I had climbed the mountain, but I wasn't enjoying the view.

It was a paralyzing reality. But even more petrifying was the fact that I didn't want to turn back. It had taken me six years of intense university study to climb this mountain. It was time for me to finally face a very hard truth in my life: *I had become a veterinarian to satisfy everyone around me.*

I've found that veterinarians can be split into two categories: those who have always had a deep-seated desire to become one, and those who find the profession later. Those in the first group would light up at the classic question, "Did you always know that you wanted to be a veterinarian since you were a kid?" whereas I would be left feeling a bit uneasy.

I loved animals and the idea of becoming a veterinarian was intellectually interesting, but it didn't fire me up to my core. The one thing I knew with absolute certainty was that I wanted to be liked.

And everyone loves a veterinarian!

Something that contributed to this was the romanticization of our profession. You see it on the television, feel it, and hear it whenever you talk to someone who is not in the industry about it.

But the problem here is this: *Frustration exists when there is a gap between expectation and reality.* And the space between the two is what trips veterinarians up when they enter their careers. That gap tripped me up, anyway.

I had been so focused on something like the excitement of an early morning C-section that I never considered that our hometown vet probably slept for only two hours, did a full day of work, and went to more emergency calls that same night.

I only saw all the good things about the career, like the fact that veterinarians got to play with puppies and kittens. There were so many things I wasn't aware of that happen beneath the surface.

After looking behind the curtain and realizing this issue was something people weren't talking about, I wondered, *How many others out there are like me? How many others are frustrated because they didn't know about this?*

These questions are precisely why I co-founded and co-host *The Veterinary Project* podcast, which aims to help veterinarians navigate their career,[1] and why I decided to write this book. With 10 years of clinical veterinary experience under my belt, I now know so much more about the profession and lifestyle that I didn't know before. My goal is to share some of this knowledge—not so that you feel the need to leave the profession, but so you can make the most out of both it and your life. I don't want to scare you off or for you to come to resent it; the truth is, even though working in veterinary medicine is hard and frustrating at times, it can also offer some of the greatest rewards known to humankind.

I simply want you to go into the rest of your life and career with intention, be better able to manage your frustrations as they arise, and be equipped with the wide range of skills necessary in this profession. I hope the experience I share in this book will help you to do just that.

At the same time, your journey is about more than simply your career. What we've come to know as "soft skills" are essential in veterinary medicine, but this label makes them seem inadequate compared to "hard skills." I now refer to them as "transferable skills" because they are so important for your career as a vet, but also in your personal life. They are some of the most valuable in this profession.

You are about to learn about the hidden challenges that come with being a veterinarian, including physical and emotional exhaustion, decision fatigue, empathy fatigue, moral distress, handling a large volume of clients, managing your identity, financial burdens, and more. This book will give you tactical ways to navigate these problems so you can minimize them and lead a more fulfilling life.

I also address "retirement" and the trajectory of your life. The days of punching the clock for 35 years and hoping to save enough money to live comfortably are over, at least where veterinarians are concerned. For me, that's meant a more unconventional path that involves real estate investing. For you, that could mean any number of things. I hope this book inspires you to think differently about financial freedom, too.

Lastly, my main intention is to positively impact people, which is why we won't spend too much time stuck in the problem and will focus instead on the solution. My goal is that by the time you've finished reading, you'll have both an awareness of the challenges in this profession that most don't know about, and the tools to navigate them in the best way possible.

I had to learn these lessons the hard way, but that doesn't mean you have to.

Chapter Two

The Paradox of Perfectionism

"HELLO, MY NAME is Mike, and I am a perfectionist." I can almost picture myself making that introduction to a group of strangers, all sitting in a circle.

I still remember hovering like a vulture around the appointment book during the early days of my veterinary career. I'd scan ahead to see what cases were coming in and strategically plan my day—but not to cherry-pick the most lucrative cases. No, I was looking for cases to dodge. Difficult cases that challenged me, that had a chance of going wrong. I wanted to avoid all of the "good" discomfort that would actually push me toward growth.

But what I was really looking for was a little space. A little time to breathe and gather my thoughts. A place to hide. And back when you needed to develop X-rays, dark rooms were the perfect place to do just that. I was looking for cases that would require radiographs.

First, let me say this: there is a beautiful dichotomy to perfectionism.

It can be a great thing in appropriate doses, like in surgery. If you were to be awake on the table, you'd probably be pretty relieved to see your surgeon has their instruments lined up in the most meticulous way and moves around the surgical field robotically (funnily enough, that was exactly what I did).

It's also incredibly useful on the path to veterinarian school. These types of schools accept a low percentage of students, so they're bound to pick people who often have near perfect report cards.

And when these students get to vet school, their perfectionism is further ingrained by the demands of the program—a rigorous program demands, and arguably breeds, perfectionists. You must have a high standard and the attention to detail to succeed. In many ways, perfectionism got us to where we are today.

Ultimately, perfectionism allowed me to become a great veterinarian and a great surgeon. Heck, you might even feel grateful for your perfectionism. I know I am in many ways.

Our sentiments toward perfectionism don't have to be so black and white, "good" or "bad," but they do become a problem in the extremes. For example, the perfectionist in me would re-inspect and overanalyze the closed incisions repeatedly during surgery—almost obsessively. If I saw the smallest bit of tissue out of alignment, it would bother me until I'd seen enough cases to flush it from my memory.

My expectations for myself were unrelenting and exhausting, but, worst of all, they were impossible to meet on a consistent basis.

The Rules Change

Perfectionism appears to run rampant in veterinary medicine, which makes a lot of sense.[2]

If you think about it, universities only admit students who have very high academic standards, so you end up with people like me—people who would get a near perfect score but can't focus on anything other than the points they missed.

When these intense efforts are isolated to shorter periods of time, such as going through vet school, they can yield incredible results (like becoming a veterinarian). This is an example of *adaptive perfectionism* at work, a type of perfectionism that is helpful and something we should all strive for. The catch is that the perfectionism doesn't end when we graduate. Rather, vet students push and push and push until they become a vet, but all the while, school has reinforced and possibly magnified a pattern of behaviors until *maladaptive perfectionism* is born.[3] This is also why I chose to start this book with perfectionism; it is the first hurdle faced by new vets, and it needs to be contained.

Adaptive perfectionism often slips into maladaptive perfectionism following veterinary school, and I believe this happens because the boundaries and limits are taken away. In other words, vet school is defined: there's correct answers, textbooks, processes, and solutions.

But after graduation the circumstances and rules of the game change. There's no defined end date in your career as a vet, no graduation to mark a finish line. There is also no defined volume of work, no "X" numbers of classes and "X" numbers of tests each semester. You can't just circle "C" and be definitively correct.

Perfectionism can therefore evolve into a crippling cycle that starts with vets thinking they need to be perfect, stressing and depleting themselves while they try to live up to that perfection, and ultimately failing at doing so—without knowing how to accept that failure. Instead, perfectionists continually try to live up to that impossible identity.

Unfortunately, it's unsustainable, especially in a profession where elements of risk and plain luck play into every procedure.

When perfectionists try to apply an exceptionally high standard to a profession where there's an unrelenting volume of work with an infinite time horizon, they simply can't keep up. It becomes inevitable that they will burn out or, at the very least, stop growing and developing if some of those factors aren't changed.

This is why it's critical that veterinarians get a handle on their perfectionism as soon as possible. *The skills that got you to the point of being a vet aren't the same skills you need for a long and healthy career.*

Imposter Syndrome

One way perfectionism manifests is imposter syndrome—and if you don't get a hold on it, it can be all-consuming and limiting to your professional growth.

A Verywell Mind article defines imposter syndrome as "an internal experience of believing that you are not as competent as others perceive you to be. While this definition is usually narrowly applied to intelligence and achievement, it has links to perfectionism and the social context."[4] Imposter syndrome is not a disease, despite the fact we often refer to it as a syndrome. Imposter syndrome is a feeling and a belief.

One 2020 study found that imposter syndrome affects around 68% of veterinarians.[5] I believe imposter syndrome is so prevalent in the veterinary community because perfectionism is too—and when you strive for perfection 100% of the time, it's easy to feel like you do not belong and must continually prove yourself. Personally, I spent most of my time in veterinarian school believing I had been admitted by mistake, which resulted in me feeling like I wasn't nearly as good as my colleagues at anything. Eventually,

I became paranoid that someone would come along, expose this truth about me, and my life would fall apart.

I was my own worst critic, and these unrelenting negative thoughts would lead me to the dark room time and time again.

Something that helped minimize my imposter syndrome was "the cat and the cow"—both of which also happen to be my favorite animals. When I was practicing, I used to love intubating cats (I know it sounds weird, but bear with me!). I'm sure you remember how wrinkly the cat's nose would get as someone held their mouth open for the E-tube—it's neat, right?

Now, when you're facing imposter syndrome, you're spiraling into your feelings and getting lost in a narrative that isn't logical or true. When this happens, I want you to think of a cat's nose wrinkling upwards and wrinkle yours the same way. Maybe you'll even laugh at yourself for a second!

This tactic works because it's a ridiculous thought and motion that snaps you out of your thinking and brings you back to the present moment—it stops the spiraling. The second thing I want you to do is take a deep breath—just like a cat does when it's intubated. Get present and breathe.

Now that you've been snapped out of the emotional spiral that comes with imposter syndrome, you can get rational with yourself. Picture yourself working with a cow. The worst place you can be is two feet behind the cow because it's such a huge animal and the biggest danger comes from getting kicked. You may recall being told to get as close to the cow you're treating as possible, even touching it, right?

Remember this: Just as you *lean into* the cow, I want you to lean into imposter syndrome.

Talk to other people about it. Reach out to friends and family and colleagues. Acknowledge what you're facing and seek help with it. The worst thing you could do with imposter syndrome, like a cow, is to withdraw from it. Imposter syndrome is like a devious little creature that exists in the darkness and scampers around your feet. It loves it when you run to the darkness and hide because it thrives there, but it cannot exist when you shine light on it.

The last thing I want you to do is evaluate *evidence* and *emotion*. Think of all the evidence that brought you to this specific point in your life: how many years you spent in school, every patient you've seen, and every surgery you've done. Whenever I opened up about my imposter syndrome to my mentor, he would ask me, "If you were on trial for being an imposter, what evidence would there be to convict you?" Of course, if the evidence is telling you you're not competent enough in something to do it proficiently, then that's good feedback and a suggestion that you need more training. But the evidence usually sways in the other direction: you're not an imposter. It's just your emotions trying to convince you that you are.

Note: When using this method, you may find you compare yourself to others you follow on social media. Be cautious about doing this, as it's *false evidence*. It's easy to see everyone's highlight reels on social media and think, *I'm not successful enough*, or *I'm not doing enough*, but that is not the case. Those lives are curated—much more is excluded from them than is included.

Lastly, when you feel a tug of imposter syndrome, I want you to think, "Good!" Don't indulge in any of the spiralling, but notice just for a moment that it showed up. This is an indicator that you are on the right path. It is an indicator of growth. The evidence suggests that you are more than capable of becoming fully competent and confident around whatever is triggering you. I am far more concerned about the veterinarian that never experiences imposter syndrome than I am for one that continually experiences it but properly navigates it.

Now that we've focused on imposter syndrome, we're going to pull back and inspect its looming cousin: perfectionism.

Facing Failure

In every veterinarian's career, there are moments they'll remember forever.

I learned this early in my career in one of the most devastating ways possible, yet, by all accounts, it was a very normal day. The morning surgeries were all wrapped up, all the medical cases were under control, and, after a lunch break, we started to pick up the typical array of vaccinations and medical appointments.

But then I heard a voice down the hall, screaming my name and I immediately knew something was wrong. I felt my entire body clench up as I racked my brain for an answer to, *What did I do?*

One of my technicians came flying into the treatment room, shock and panic on her face. Wanting to avoid a scene, she didn't say anything besides, "Follow me. Quickly."

As I ran behind her towards the kennel room, a massive lump grew in my throat, and suddenly, I felt like I couldn't breathe. My heart was racing, and with each step closer toward the kennel room it pounded louder in my ears. When I turned the corner and she opened the door, I held back my gaze for as long as I could. I didn't want to look.

My head dropped as she told me what I already knew: "He's dead."

It took me some time to recognize the dog, but only because he was in the clinic for an extremely mundane procedure:

a straight-forward neuter. It was a procedure I had done close to a hundred times at that point in my career. Even worse, I didn't have the slightest hint that anything went less than perfectly. And, based on his records, the 18-month-old dog was very healthy, so my mind started racing through all the possible reasons he had died.

I stopped averting my eyes and looked at the motionless dog. Sheer panic set in as I approached him. Part of me wanted to run and hide, but I knew I was the veterinarian and all responsibility landed on me.

I placed a stethoscope on the dog and listened closely, but there was no heartbeat. I held on a little longer—realistically knowing that the dog was already dead, but hoping desperately that it wasn't true. Hoping that, somehow, I could will the heart to beat again. I thought, *Maybe she's wrong. Maybe his heart is still beating.* But after a few more moments of listening, I confirmed the truth. Later, a post-mortem exam would reveal that the dog's death was 100% a surgical error. The ligatures that I had placed over the spermatic blood vessels had slipped off and caused the dog to internally bleed to death.

That moment became what was unquestionably the worst day of my veterinary career, but, in hindsight, it was also one of my most pivotal moments because of *what I learned.*

How to Manage Perfectionism

Before that surgery, I had been told numerous times that, sooner or later, I would have a patient pass away unintentionally. But that didn't change the fact that having a patient unintentionally pass away under *my* care was my ultimate fear—and what I believed would be my ultimate failure.

That day I experienced my worst fear...but I also got through it. Surviving that moment meant I could survive anything because I had a new perspective on failure. I was finally able to accept that I was going to continue to fail time and time again, live through it, and grow because of it. That consistently achieving perfection was impossible.

This mindset is crucial because it doesn't just apply to veterinary medicine—it also applies to life! In tandem with this new perspective, I began to develop more strategies that helped me manage my imposter syndrome and perfectionism along with other struggles I was facing. I call these my *core tenets*.

If you really want to start living and free yourself from the burden of unmanaged perfectionism, these core tenets will help:

- **Continually lead with gratitude.** Perfectionists spend a lot of time and energy fixated on meeting their standards and chasing their goals. In Dan Sullivan's book with Benjamin Hardy, *The Gap and The Gain: The High Achievers' Guide to Happiness, Confidence, and Success*, the authors outline your goal self, your present self, and your past self, and the distance between them.[6] The "gap" is the distance between your goal self and present self, whereas the "gain" is the distance between your past self and your present self. This model allows you to constantly focus on what is good and what is working—in other words, looking at the "gain" and not the "gap." Sullivan and Hardy even suggest that the reader "measure backwards," whereas us veterinarians are always thinking about what we haven't done yet (e.g. *I have one more surgery left today*) instead of thinking about what we've already accomplished (e.g. *I've finished four surgeries today*).[7] Another way of looking at this idea links back to the "cow" from earlier in this chapter. If you live in the gap, you will get kicked in the face by the cow. Focus instead on your gains and acknowledge your achievements with gratitude.

- **Adopt a growth mindset.** There is an element of risk and luck to everything, but oftentimes, a perfectionist will limit themselves by sticking to what's in their comfort zone out of fear that they will mess up anything beyond that. Instead of restricting yourself, I suggest you take on the attitude that *mistakes are there for you to learn and grow from.* Letting go of mistakes doesn't mean that you don't care or that you're a bad vet, it simply means that you accept mistakes are part of growth. Furthermore, failure can get us down if we focus only on the result and not the effort. But what if we focussed on our inputs instead? *What did you put into it? What did you learn? What did you get right?* This is the difference between leads (your effort, what is in your control) and lags (the results). For example, say you're trying to lose weight—you can only control what you eat, how much you exercise you do, and the effort you put in. You cannot directly change the number on the scale. You do know, though, that if you keep focusing on the leads, the lags will follow.

- **Define your *why*.** A strong *why* is what will guide you when you face a setback—a directive to fall back on. In your darkest moments, whenever things look grim and hopeless, a strong *why* will keep you focused on the bigger picture and inspired to push past any temporary failure. In the process of defining your *why*, make sure your *why* is uniquely yours—don't rely on anyone else for external validation (as perfectionists have a tendency to do). You are on your own journey, which you must honor.

It took me quite a long time to accept these core tenets, but when I did, my outlook on life changed. I became curious again, ready to embrace whatever challenges were thrown my way. I stopped judging the past because I felt like I could breathe again. When you too begin to grasp these concepts, you'll be able to see the silver lining of failure instead of being stuck in a restrictive perfectionist headspace.

No one puts it better than early business theorist Arthur Sheldon, but it was brought to my attention by the brilliant personal development author and speaker Earl Nightingale: "Success is the progressive realization of a worthy ideal." The key word here is *progressive*. It's the process that's important, not any one individual event.

One of Those Moments

After leaving the kennel room, I was completely rattled and unable to focus on anything else. I felt terrible for the poor dog, was dreading breaking the news to the owners, and was embarrassed beyond belief. I wanted to crawl into a ball and disappear forever.

Thankfully, everyone at the clinic was incredibly supportive and other vets shared stories of the times their patients had unexpectedly passed. One of the most helpful pieces of advice I received was a three-step process to bounce back from mistakes. I still use this format all the time, whether it's for small errors or bigger failures.

1. **Apologize and own the mistake.** Don't ever try to make an excuse or brush it off.

2. **Do the right thing.** In the case of my surgical error, we covered the cost of a third-party post-mortem and provided full transparency to the owner. You can't always make things whole, but you can always do what you know is right.

3. **Go one step further.** The dog that passed away was a trained German Shepherd guard dog, so without hesitation, my clinic bought a similar dog for the client and took care of all of its first year of life needs. We went over and beyond anything the owner could have reasonably expected.

As veterinarians, we are in a position of some level of control over life and death—a powerful privilege. On one hand, you have the ability and the tools to make an incredible difference in the outcome and quality of life for your patients, but on the other, there is so much that could—and does—go wrong.

Most people will never have both the opportunity to contribute *and* the opportunity to fail in this way. You see, you cannot have one without the other. If you want to be in a position where you can make hugely positive impacts, you have to also carry the burden of doing the opposite.

But that is just part of life—and how we choose to deal with our mistakes is what matters.

In my case, the client fortunately accepted the new dog and the care we offered, but with one caveat. When the new dog was to be neutered, they specifically requested it wasn't me doing the surgery!

It was a fair trade-off, but I know I gained much more from this experience than I could've imagined. I can say with 100% certainty that I thought about this exact surgery *every single time* before I made my opening cut on every neuter I performed for the rest of my career. As a result, I evaluated my surgical technique, choice of suture, and ligature patterns and made adjustments. I immediately became a better surgeon.

This event permanently shaped how I show up in all areas of life and business. Mistakes were reframed as an opportunity to review what is working and what is not, and to get better.

Looking back on this event over a decade later, I can absolutely and unequivocally say that one of my greatest failures was simultaneously one of my biggest steps forward.

The Paradox of Relationships

We've talked about failure and how it's OK to make mistakes—but I want to reiterate that there can be some benefit to making them. I didn't realize it back in the day, but along with making mistakes can come a pleasant surprise: an opportunity to *improve* relationships. My experience has largely been that the handling of the mistake is often more impactful on the relationship than the actual making of the mistake.

The reason why you should cherish these opportunities to do better is because relationships are *everything* in veterinarian medicine. Dr. Kent Weir, who was one of our first guests on *The Veterinary Project* podcast, echoed this statement through the wise words of his grandfather (who was also a vet): "Veterinary medicine is service industry. It's about the people. Behind every animal, is a person."[8]

Ultimately, if you make a mistake, use it as an opportunity to show up for another person.

At the same time, there is a paradox here that ties into being a perfectionist. As a vet student, you received so much of your validation externally—whenever you passed a test, achieved something, or even when you got your degree—and that validation continued when you became a new vet. Many people within the clinic probably praised you in the beginning, and so did your clients.

The problem here comes from building relationships based solely on external validation. S.D. Buffington in *The Law of Abundance* summarizes it nicely:

"The problem is we can't discover who we are by directing our attention 'out there.' When we do that, the messages are always mixed, and we can never become enough. It is not possible to please all the people all the time, and if our sense of self revolves around other people's opinions, we are doomed to a life of striving."[9]

Essentially, a perfectionist could experience the paradox of relationships because of their desire to meet standards placed on them by those same relationships. Now that you're aware of this trap, don't fall into it—instead, strive towards developing a strong sense of self-confidence and self-worth so that you can better navigate this paradox.

The Process Builds Confidence

At this point, we've discussed how a veterinarian's perfectionism can result in fear of failure and looked at some techniques that can help you manage perfectionism and imposter syndrome. But where do we go from there?

Let's talk about one of the by-products of embracing these core tenets: confidence.

You see, it's not enough to just accept that failure is going to happen. You want to be able to live in a state where you accept that reality and are *still confident enough* to move forward.

What I really want you to grasp is that due to the years of schooling that you've had, you are *highly* competent. My veterinary mentor always used to say to me, "The problem is confidence, not competence." And if I look at the evidence, I can see he was right.

If you're ever to gain confidence in an area, you have to take action in it, accept that you will make mistakes, and learn from them. It's the only way to move forward—there is no shortcut. In the words of David Joseph Schwartz, "Do what you fear, and fear disappears."[10]

And, while you're tackling your fears, learn to *love the process* because it's a beautiful one! You're developing your skills through passionate curiosity, a curiosity that leads you to rewards only available to those who have earned them in the veterinary arena.

Chapter Three

How to Eat an Elephant

THE TITLE "HOW to Eat an Elephant" is a little tongue in cheek, but there's intention behind it. In our profession, there's a tendency to be completely consumed by the work because of the volume of clients and cases we deal with. It's one wave after another that never stops.

The quality of your life will be matched by the quality of the questions you ask, and as veterinarians, we've been asking ourselves "how" to eat an elephant for far too long. It's a poor question.

The start of a song rang in my ears with the line, *I'm not trying to be your hero,* as my shoulders dropped and I inhaled a deep amount of dread. This opener would play at the same time every morning, signifying the start of a programming segment I'd listen to on the way to work. But for me, the song would signal that it was the beginning of another long and exhausting day. Reminiscent of Pavlov's dogs, I could literally feel my adrenal glands pump cortisol throughout my body whenever the song came on.

As I drove closer and closer to the clinic, my mind would race in all sorts of directions. *What if the clinic just vanished? What if*

I got into an accident? What if the power was down for the day? Of course, I didn't want any of these things to happen—I just wanted to have time away from the office without me having to raise my hand and ask for it.

One tense drive later, I huffed and sighed and pushed my way through the old, familiar steel door that was the back entrance to the clinic. After flinging the door open wide and hurrying through, the spring-loaded latch slammed it shut behind me with a loud *bang*. Everyone in the clinic knew that I had arrived.

I wouldn't have another second to breathe for the rest of the day.

Before my jacket was even off, I was swarmed with questions. This chaos would ensue throughout the morning surgeries and seep into afternoon appointments until the day ended, as always, an hour or two behind schedule.

That was my life at work and it wasn't making my life at home any better. I carried *everything* back with me.

Slowly, as my veterinarian career progressed, I changed from a relaxed, joking, and happy-go-lucky guy into a tense, stressed, shut down human being. I used to be able to walk out of the clinic door at the end of the day and completely turn off my work brain so I could enjoy my evenings and weekends, but gradually the cases started following me home. I'd come in the door and want absolutely nothing to do with anyone. No talking. No activity. I'd either zone out in front of the T.V. just to shut my brain down or fall asleep from exhaustion on the couch.

My despair affected those around me. I was treating my loved ones poorly, including my wife, Rosalie. Something as simple as a casual morning coffee would become a battleground if she even so much as asked me a question.

Everything culminated one night when I came home to my

wife. It had been a terrible day at work that ended with me coming home late, so I stared at the food in front of me intently—it was the only thing I wanted to interact with.

I heard Rosalie asking me questions in the background, but I wasn't listening at all. Finally, she placed a hand on my shoulder, gave me a bit of a squeeze, and repeated, "Mike!"

I was pulled out of my daze, but I didn't have the energy to apologize. Instead, I was all apathy.

Rosalie sensed it. For the thousandth time, I watched as that look of extreme frustration took shape on her face, the kind of look that comes with not being let in by a person you care about.

Like many of our fights at this point in my life, this one entailed me not being present, my lack of energy, and my inability to connect and engage. I shook my head in denial, but that was just to hide the fact that I knew she was right. Also, as usual, I attempted to conclude the discussion by putting up a wall and hoping the problem would go away.

But what she said next finally got through to me.

Flustered and exasperated, she looked at me and exclaimed, "Mike...you're miserable! You are Miserable Mike!" as if that was my villain name (and, in a way, it kind of was). Rosalie and I had been living together for several years when this happened, so if anyone knew me well, it was her.

Hearing my new moniker Miserable Mike hit me hard. All at once, the reality sunk in that such a negative state had become my new normal. It was no longer just a bad day or a bad mood—my entire personality had done a 180.

That day I realized three very important things: That I was miserable. That I was hurting those I loved. And that I didn't want to be miserable anymore. Everything changed that day.

When I reflect on Miserable Mike, I try to think about how

I got there. How did I get so far away from who I wanted to be for so long?

I came to the conclusion that Miserable Mike felt like he had no control over his life or happiness, but he was so wrong. I soon learned that I had to stop blaming work for my outlook. *I was 100% responsible for my life*, and it was time to do something about it.

I started by tackling the sheer volume of my daily tasks, which I felt was one of the biggest attributors to my constant feeling of drowning at work. I was trying to do so many things and see so many patients every day, but was constantly failing by not meeting the impossible expectations I had set for myself—just like the obsessive perfectionist I was. On top of that, I was going home to a long list of non-work-related tasks to get through. I always felt like I didn't have enough capacity, or space on my plate, to manage everything I needed to throughout the day.

When I finally began to manage the volume problem, it felt like I had just uncovered some major secret. It had been affecting *everything*. When volume was under control, every other problem I was facing suddenly became easier to navigate.

All vets can benefit in some way by taking control of their volume. When you go through a system that trains you to become a perfectionist, it's only natural that you'll want to see every client and help every pet.

But my hope is that every vet's hours, capacity, and volume will eventually look different because, honestly, they should. We are not all the same, so no solution or schedule should be the same.

And in doing so, we will finally break the cycle of veterinarians feeling like they have to work 60 plus hours a week just because that's what the previous generation of vets did.

To avoid becoming Miserable *Your-Name-Here*, I want you to know that you *do* have control over this aspect of work. In this chapter, I'm going to show you techniques to help you tackle the endless stream of appointments.

Maslow's Hierarchy of Needs

Where do Miserable *Fill-in-the-Blank*s come from?

In retrospect, I can now see that I was in pure survival mode. When you're in this state, you're not living intentionally and you feel unable to change anything in your life—kind of like you're running on a perpetual hamster wheel.

We can compare this to Maslow's Hierarchy of Needs:

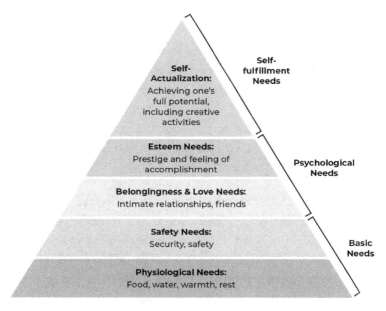

I was stuck on the bottom tier.

When you get caught in this zone, you have no energy for

higher-up levels (that include your relationships and friends). You also have no chance of reaching self-actualization when survival is all that matters, so your growth as an individual is stagnated.

This sentiment doesn't just apply to me. Time and time again, other vets have described to me the feeling of being in pure survival mode. This is a huge issue because those in pure survival mode tend to fear slowing down or resting because they believe their whole world will crash if they do. The problem is, if you don't ever slow down, life will *make* you slow down at some point. For me, the catalyst for change came from desperation, but it doesn't have to play out that way for you.

The good news is that, as vets, we are problem-solvers. That means you don't need a playbook detailing *how* you're going to make a change—all you need to do is recognize that change is necessary. Something everyone does need, however, is some space to gain clarity. And, in a way, that's what Rosalie gave me when she called me Miserable Mike. It was the wakeup call that gave me just enough room to step back and finally see what was going on. You need to take that space too, and you don't need permission to take it. But be warned, if you do recognize this issue in yourself and do nothing to change it, you are essentially choosing to accept it.

Quality of Life

It is my personal belief that the volume of work in veterinary medicine is perhaps the single greatest threat to a veterinarian's health and well-being. I've heard time and time again from veterinarians that most of their fatigue comes from sheer volume and intensity. Furthermore, mental work is just as, if not more, energy-consuming than physical work. The catch is that many veterinarians find themselves in roles that are both mentally *and* physically demanding. Being a vet is not the same as doing a physical job that requires no thinking or a "desk" job that requires no movement: clinical vets do both!

So here are my tips to combatting the problem, which we dive into further below:

- Shift Your Perspective

- Quit Relying on Your Income

- Get Intentional

By embracing these points you will experience less fatigue and burnout and gain more time to recharge. Your mind will be fresher for all critical decisions you have to make, and you will be able to offer more empathetic care for patients. It sounds counterintuitive but taking these steps will ultimately make you a better vet—while still providing a better life for yourself and those you care about.

1. **Shift Your Perspective**

When you hear the word *success*, what comes to mind?

For most people, it would be the seemingly complementary words *money*, or *career status*. Somehow, things have progressed in this world so that the two are synonymous, and people who work absurdly long days and get two hours of sleep are the ones "doing it right."

Unfortunately, veterinarians aren't free from this trap either. In veterinary medicine, the traditional model seems to be that you need to work well over 50 hours a week in order to be "successful." The only thing this does is lead to a lot of frustration, burnout, and sleepless nights.

On both an individual and industry-wide level, we've been trying to eat the elephant because "that's the way it has always been," which is also indictive of the large gap in attitude between those who are retiring now and those who are at the beginning of their careers. Thankfully, we've seen things change time and time again in our world. From computers to phones to email, we know that progress can be a good thing—so why not encourage it in our industry?

That being said, change is much easier said than done— but it starts with you and your perspective.

Shifting your outlook on success will happen when you conquer your inner voice. We will look into this more in a later chapter on identity, but it comes down to reframing the internal voices that tell you, "I am not enough," "I can handle it all," or, "My worth comes from my professional performance."

In order to make peace with the caseload that is right for you, these are the questions you will ultimately need to ask yourself (and answer honestly): *Who am I doing this for?* and *What am I ultimately trying to accomplish?*

Remember, unlike veterinary school, there is no end in sight when it comes to clinical volume. In practice, you have to get up every morning and do it all over again. You might as well change what your day looks like so it works for you.

2. **Quit Relying on Your Income**

Dr. Dan Katz, a guest on *The Veterinary Project* podcast put it well when he said, "If you rely on something, you will eventually grow to resent it."[11]

It seems so obvious that the number one answer to combatting overwhelming volume is to reduce that volume (because it is). If you can solve this problem, you will gain your freedom back and get yourself out of survival mode. To be clear, this will be a gradual process. Little by little, things will change with the ultimate goal to partially or completely replace your income so you can get out of survival mode.

Because nothing sets you free like not needing a paycheque.

It is my belief that every veterinarian should try to replace their veterinary income with multiple sources of passive income. I know this sounds like a big stretch and may even be an overwhelming idea, but you can start anywhere. (Don't worry, we will look at how you can start making passive income in a later chapter.)

When I first started out in real estate, my goal was to continually cut back the number of hours I worked as a vet while maintaining the same overall amount of income. I was basically buying my time back and working only when I wanted to. This has evolved into my greatest vision for veterinarian medicine: a world where veterinarians earn enough money and have the financial stability to be able to work part-time (or an amount of their choosing). We do such mentally and physically intense work that a part-time schedule can be enough (along with some form of passive income)—and, to be frank, that's where the industry is heading.

Of course, how much you want to buy into this idea is up to you. However, it will be very difficult to solve the volume problem as long as you're fully dependent on your full-time veterinarian income.

(Note: Charge for what you do. Vets are notorious discounters, but every time a vet chooses to discount by 10%, they are electing to double their volume. If you want to reduce volume, quit discounting and charge in full for the work you do.)

3. Get Intentional

Many veterinarians find themselves in a state of survival,

constantly having to react to whatever is thrown their way. The day just happens to them and they respond as best they can.

The problem is that if you're always just reacting, you're always behind.

When you take charge of your day, everything changes. Suddenly you have enough time to breathe. To think deeply about your intentions rather than being rushed. To make the most efficient use of your time.

If you want to stop reacting, focus on these three things:

1. Gratitude

2. Planning

3. Boundaries

Gratitude is vital because it focuses your reticular activating system (RAS), that bundle of neurons in your brain stem tasked with filtering inputs, in the right direction. When you tell your RAS to look out for things to be grateful for, it will filter through the endless stimuli that you encounter on a daily basis and present to you…more things to be grateful for!

As veterinarians, we have a tremendous amount to be grateful for—like the ability to save lives, bring people joy, and do some real good in the world. All we have to do is *see it that way*. One way I remind myself of this is by doing a five minute "gratitude journal" every day, where I focus on a number of things I'm grateful for.

Of course, it can be hard to be grateful when you're working long days and seeing challenging cases, but if you work on "rewiring" your brain to focus on the good, you'll identify a lot more opportunities to be grateful.

Planning. When I was in university, I heard a story about a professor who, in class, started to drop some big rocks into a container, and then some smaller rocks to fill in the open cracks and spaces. He asked his students if the container was full, and they agreed it was—but then he poured some sand in. The sand filled in all the rest of the little gaps. He asked again if the container was full, to which they replied, "Yes." Finally, he poured some water in, which filled the rest of the container up. The lesson here being that we need to put the big pieces in first—if we planned backwards instead—or did not plan at all—there would be no room in the container for the big rocks.

Planning, therefore, is helpful in managing volume in two ways: firstly, it helps to know what big things are coming your way, and secondly, it lets you see the big picture. It's about putting attention and intention into where we give our energy and time.

For me, this all started with a book. Very few books really change a person's life, but *The Miracle Morning* by Hal Elrod completely changed mine.

If you had told me five years ago that I would become a morning person, I would never have believed you, but that's exactly what this book allowed me to uncover in myself. I went from being a *reactionary person*—a guy who hits the snooze button—to being a *proactive person* who tackles the day with excitement.

As Elrod discusses, transitioning into the "morning person" type isn't just about gaining an hour in the morning to get a head start on your day—in fact, the "miracle morning" doesn't have to be in the morning at all. It can take place whenever you start your day. For a shift worker, for instance, this could be your "miracle afternoon" or "miracle evening."[12]

Instead, the start of your day is a time to completely focus on yourself, separate from the outside world. In the quiet of dawn, the goal is to be very intentional about the day you intend to create for yourself before all the demands of the outside world start flooding in.

It may be a cliché, but this is how you set yourself up to achieve whatever your definition of success is. I recommend you pick up a copy of *The Miracle Morning* yourself, but just to give you an idea, below were the most helpful things I learned from that book.

- **Gratitude:** approaching everything with a grateful attitude can have a huge impact on your perspective (as discussed earlier).

- **Exercise:** taking care of your body and health in the morning sets you up for the same the rest of the day. For me, getting outside is also extremely powerful.

- **Visualization:** I regularly write down and capture how I want my life to feel. I then read back what I wrote and afterwards, I close my eyes and visualize it.

- **Reading:** every morning, I focus my mind on areas I want to learn about and improve in through reading.

- **Quiet Reflection:** Elrod calls this "Silence," but for me, it's mindfulness.[13]

Just as important as what I do is what I *don't* do: I stay off the T.V., internet, social media, news, and email. The goal of my miracle morning is to aim the first hour of my day in the direction I choose—not toward what the world wants me to pay attention to.

Finally, **boundaries**. We work in a profession that makes it very difficult to say "No" when you're constantly seeing pets in pain and have an endless stream of clients. Knowing how to do so—in a professional and constructive way—will help tremendously with volume. We will tackle ways to set boundaries in Chapter 8.

In and Out

I want to note here that there are two ways that volume has an impact: in our career and in our personal life. Not only do we have a ton of demands coming from our career, we also have demands in our personal life as a husband, wife, partner, parent, son, daughter, friend etc.

Knowing this fact doesn't solve the issue, but it's important to recognize it. I want you to acknowledge that these many facets of your life work in tandem and understand that the need to manage your volume will happen in many areas of your life (in fact, many of the volume-reducing techniques we've talked about so far can just as successfully be applied to your personal life as to your career). Crucially, you will find that managing volume in one area of your life can contribute to success in another!

Let the Elephant Roam

There's a fable about two men. One, a shop owner, watches as the other man stops outside his window every morning, looks up, and continues on. Meanwhile, the shopkeeper wonders why the man keeps stopping outside his store until he hears the factory whistle go off at 5 o'clock. He adjusts his clock, closes his store, and goes home.

The same thing happens every day.

After watching this go on for months, the shopkeeper finally decides to talk to the man. When he sees him outside his window, he runs outside and asks him, "Hey! Why do you stop outside my store every morning?"

The man responds, "I'm the foreman at the factory. I blow the 5 o'clock whistle, so it's really important that I get the time right."

"Oh," the shopkeeper replies, "I set my clock based on the sound of the factory whistle."

Neither man really knew what time it was, and both assumed the other knew the actual time. Each man was just following the follower.

Part of the reason volume is such an issue in veterinary medicine is because we're all just following the follower. When we were starting out, we heard, "I worked long days so you have to too," from more experienced vets. Taking on a high volume almost became a rite of passage.

I wish an industry-wide rehaul could be done, but failing that, the responsibility has to fall to each and every one of us to set our own limits and take care of our personal well-being. If your goal is to practice for many years, then your workload simply *needs* to be adjusted. Trust me when I say you will accomplish much less in a 10-year career going all out than in a 30-year one where you pace yourself.

All this is to say, there's really no point in asking how to eat the elephant. A better question to ask that leads to a more nuanced and helpful answer and therefore a higher quality of life would be, *Why should I bother to eat one anyway?*

Chapter Four

Decisions Dictate Your Life

I F YOU HAD asked me in 2018 what my favorite part of being a veterinarian was, well, I probably would have ripped your head off for asking me one more damn question! That, or completely shut down and ignored you.

Oftentimes, it was impossible to feel like I had anything left to give at the end of the day, because everyone would want a piece of me. I would just want to be left alone. When you experience decision fatigue, any additional questions set you off.

I always wish I had done an experiment where I counted every single decision I made in a day as a practicing veterinarian. I imagine using one of those clickers to count them, but know it would stall out at the maximum number.

If you think about it, veterinarians make an absurd number of decisions a day; we must make all of the same decisions as most adults, which is approximately 35,000 for the average adult,[14] but we're also in a profession where we are the solution providers to problems. The sheer volume of decisions we must make is intense: we're constantly having rapid-fire questions tossed at us from all levels—clients, colleagues, staff, phone calls, texts, emails, and even through social media. Some of these decisions are relatively insignificant but confronting bigger decisions can make you feel like the entire world is depending on you. Add to that, the level of responsibility (consequences) attached to these decisions is sometimes life and death.

Decision fatigue is likely affecting vets in a negative way. It caused me to carry a heavy weight in my life for a long time, and it's probably a burden in yours too.

But as a doctor, many people turn to you—even if the client ultimately has to own the decision.

This means we must evolve the way we think about and handle decision-making. Rather than dread the process, let's not only take back some of the control, but also recognize decision-making as the valuable skill that it is. Make no mistake about it, those that reach the highest levels in their careers and personal lives are effective decision-makers! That being said, the intention behind this chapter is not to "solve" decision fatigue, because that's not really possible. The goal is to instead give you some tools that can make dealing with decisions more manageable.

Decision-Making Is a Muscle

Decision-making in the veterinary clinic doesn't just spontaneously happen.

We have been training and reinforcing our decision-making process throughout our entire life, and, just like any muscle, our decision-making ability fatigues with repetition throughout the day. That means to conserve our energy we need to make fewer decisions and/or use less energy with each decision we make.

With a few organizational efforts, you can get this muscle in top shape, while also avoiding any unnecessary strain on it. Let's start with some of the basics:

1. **Automate whenever possible.** This is sound advice for those of us for whom the sheer volume of decisions is the primary source of stress. In other words, just reduce the number of those tasks. For instance, set up a recurring calendar event rather than inputting it each time, or hire a trainer to plan your workouts so you don't have to think about a thing. Don't underestimate how taking care of the little things conserves energy to tackle the big things.

2. **Ruthlessly eliminate.** In Chapter 3 we talked about the importance of being strategic about volume so you can reserve your capacity. Similarly, you need to be strategic about your choices so you can reserve your decision-making ability. That means cutting all low-level tasks and choices from your day, like how Steve Jobs chose to wear his classic black shirt day after day...there's nothing left to decide. Also, look for "root cause decisions" wherever possible—in other words, make one decision that eliminates all other downstream decisions. An example is meal-planning in advance and choosing *not* to buy junk food at the grocery store. That way you only need to make that decision once versus if you brought home random groceries and looked at them a hundred times, trying to decide whether or not to eat them each time.

3. **Delegate when you can.** When you can't eliminate or automate, delegate. This falls in line with reducing the sheer number of decisions you make a day. Empower the amazing team around you and remember that vet techs can do a lot (oftentimes, even better than we can)! Trust them to make decisions when appropriate. And building off the grocery example above, imagine fully delegating your meal planning and grocery shopping to a professional cook or

meal delivery service. Now you never need to stare down a bag of chips and burn up precious decision-making energy.

4. **Plan ahead.** It makes sense that knowing exactly what you're doing on a daily basis can help automate your life. Sometimes, we refer to this as *bookending*, which we will explore further in Chapter 9. Bookending can greatly serve you because it creates closure in advance—once a scheduled decision is fully made and committed to, it carries no lingering weight. For instance, to make exercising easier, I plan out my weeks on Sundays so that I don't have to make any workout decisions mid-week. My workouts are also planned by a trainer, so exercise consumes none of my decision-making energy during the week.

5. **Run into the fire.** Do you know you're going to have to make a tough decision today? Instead of putting it off until the last moment, tackle it early in the day. First, you are not yet fatigued, so you will likely make a better decision. Second, putting a decision off will eat away at your energy because it will still sit in the back of your mind, nagging at you. In a clinic setting, "running into the fire" may mean reviewing your hospitalized cases, looking over treatment plans, and tackling the most difficult cases first before jumping into the flow of your regular day.

6. **Stay fueled.** Just like any cell, your brain needs energy to operate! That means you need rest and proper sustenance to operate at your optimal levels. One catch is that as we fatigue, we make poor decisions, which is why nutrition must be planned. Reaching for that sugary treat because we are fatigued is not a great substitute for a well-planned, healthy snack.

While I find these six tactical strategies to be extremely helpful, they can only get you so far, especially as a veterinarian. They have been widely talked about and most definitely work, but when you're in a niche like ours, you need to investigate further. Let's discuss why.

Indecision Fatigue

First and foremost, veterinary medicine is a service business, meaning that our clients seek out our professional guidance to give them sound advice—which is literally what they pay for. Therefore, decision-making will always be a significant part of the job. You can't just avoid or get rid of it entirely.

But in my personal clinical experience, it wasn't always the *number* of decisions I was making that exhausted me, it was the fact that I sometimes couldn't (or chose not to) make decisions and would carry them around with me all day.

Every time I had a tedious case I didn't quite know what to do with, or blood results that weren't definitive enough, it would feel like I was filling a backpack up with rocks all day long, each indecision being yet more weight on my back.

That's why the insidious next-door neighbor of decision fatigue is *indecision fatigue*, or the similar concept "analysis paralysis."

Think of how much energy you expend just to reach the point where you can make a decision as a veterinarian. You have to carefully analyze all available information, use your previous experience to provide context and perspective, and lay out all possible options for paths forward. All this takes energy, so it's critical that you make a decision after doing all of that work to advance the case forward. To be clear, the decision you make doesn't need to be the *final* decision—you don't need to know exactly what to do—but you need to know what you're doing next. For example, it's OK to make a decision to review all the information you have and sleep on something or reach out to a mentor; that's a definitive choice too! Just don't leave it open.

The alternative is setting the case down and coming back to it later. You'll just have to pick back up all the pieces you gathered earlier (patient history, test results, etc.) and do the mental decision-making work twice. In this scenario, you actually expend more energy just to end up back in the exact same spot, where the decision you didn't make earlier is still waiting for you.

All this indecision seems troublesome, but it's important to remember that indecision is also a muscle. Just as you've been forming your decision-making process your entire life, you've been shaping your indecision process as well, especially as you progressed in your veterinarian career and have had to deal with indecision much more frequently.

So, what can we do about it?

1. **Never let fear stop you from doing something.**

   In a critical moment where it's time to make a decision and you hesitate, you are very likely operating out of fear: fear of failure, fear of missing out, fear of being wrong, fear of causing harm to a patient, and even fear of your own ego.

   I don't mention this to imply that the fear isn't valid, as a great veterinarian's nature is to avoid harm (and if you do hesitate, I would explore why to ensure you aren't making a poor medical decision). But when fear is present, you are not thinking as rationally as you could.

   Next time you recognize fear is causing your indecision, assess whether the fear is real and danger is near. If it is, you can honor that fear. If it isn't, you need to put that fabricated fear aside in your mind.

2. Build the habit of quick and decisive decisions.

Creating a habit of quick and decisive decision-making is another tool for combatting indecision. You do this by starting small, in day-to-day life, where the stakes are small.

Take the dreaded, "Where are we going to eat?" question, for example. We've all been out with friends or stuck in a group message where someone asks this question and everyone's face goes blank or phones go silent. Maybe someone says, "I'm not sure, does anyone else have an idea?" while another says, "No, but I don't care where we go." It's hopeless!

If you ever find yourself in a position like this, take the opportunity to build on your quick and effective decision-making skills: I challenge you to be the first person to answer this question every time it comes up. Don't think about it too much! Others will be grateful you took the lead.

It's great to train in these low-stakes situations because the consequences are usually insignificant. For example, if you happen to go somewhere where the food isn't very good, it's no big deal. Your dinner-mates will forgive you (if they're even bothered) and you'll know to not return to that place.

After starting with small choices, you can move up to bigger ones to build the muscle. Remember, the decision-making process has parallels regardless of the consequences. The goal here is to train yourself to be quick and decisive when the consequences are low-risk, and then carry that muscle memory over into higher-stake decision-making. My hope is that you will eventually be comfortable enough with decision-making that you're never overly indecisive again!

(Note: I'm not encouraging you to *think less* when making decisions, but instead to be more decisive! Obviously, making low-stake decisions like where to go to dinner isn't likely to have negative consequences, but in high-stake decisions—like a medical decision—a life could be on the line.)

3. **Scalpel blade decisions**

I believe a useful analogy can be found in the surgical suite, so let's investigate there.

Think of the last time you picked up the scalpel blade to perform a routine abdominal surgery. Your first order of business was to make an incision into the abdominal cavity. Note the semantics there: you are "cutting into" something, or making an *in*-cision. If we were to do the opposite of this, we would be "cutting off" something, or making a *de*-cision.

These types of cuts represent the two sides of decision-making: choosing something *and* eliminating other options.

Most people don't think about the flip side of decision-making. Everyone can agree that when you make a decision, you are choosing something, but the real magic happens when you are *not* choosing everything else!

To do this, you have cut other options away—the key being to not only cut yourself off from them physically, but emotionally and energetically as well. Think of debriding the necrotic tissue on a healing wound. Once you cut it off, you throw it away! You don't hang on to it just in case you change your mind and want to suture it back on later. Doing this will force you to stop ruminating on the options you eliminated. When we hold on to them by second guessing and playing the "what if" game, they gain emotional weight over us as we replay the decision over and over in our minds, which further fatigues us!

Instead, let go of all the potential options you did not choose. Do as Michael Jordan does, in his own words: "Once I made a decision, I never thought about it again."

Our approach to decision-making should be this disciplined too. However, while I firmly believe this level of conviction is necessary in decision-making, we still need to allow room for new evidence to be introduced into medicine—we don't want to chase confirmation bias.

4. *Use The Confidence > Decision Flywheel*

Something interesting happens when you make a decision quickly and resolutely: you deliver your decision with confidence. You can hear it in your tone of voice and see it in your body language.

Back in Chapter 2, I said that confidence can't just be picked up somewhere, but that it has to be gained by taking action. Let's explore that idea further. The reason a firm, definitive decision leads to an increase in confidence is because it leads you into action. Taking action increases your confidence because you will gain new knowledge and experience from that action, which in turn empowers you to make another decision. With even more confidence, another decision can be made without reluctance, followed by another, and another!

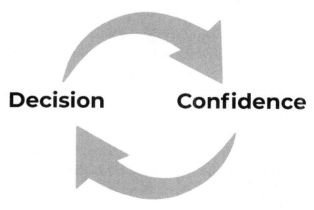

Decision   **Confidence**

Think back to a day in clinical practice (or your life) when you were fully in the zone—when you were completely *on fire*. You were able to come up with a definitive course of action for everything that came at you, you diagnosed and prescribed treatments on all sorts of cases, and next steps came to you naturally.

You may have even experienced being in a *flow state*. While there are many variations of its definition, my favorite comes from author Philip McKernan, who defined flow state to me once as, "Your body and mind being in exactly the same spot." In other words, you are totally present and engaged. Your body and thoughts are in the same rhythm, working in tandem.

So, on such an occasion, how did you feel as the day progressed?

I always felt more energetic as the day went on, but why? It didn't happen because someone slipped something special into my coffee; it happened because I was feeding off my confident decision-making.

If most of us struggle with indecision fatigue or are paralyzed by analysis, doesn't it make sense that being decisive would make you feel the opposite of fatigued? Or at the very least, considerably less fatigued?

On those extraordinary days, I probably made just as many decisions as I usually did, but I wasted no time or energy caught in the metaphorical tar of indecision. The goal is to foster this kind of mindset every day, but you need confidence to get there.

My advice is to generate that strong body language for yourself instead of waiting for it to happen. The more you make decisions in this manner, the more you will really start to believe in yourself.

It all starts with making just one decision quickly and confidently. This will create the momentum needed to break free from indecision.

Doctor of Veterinary Medicine (D.V.M.)

You may be thinking that making quick, definitive decisions is not how most of us are wired. That we need to be right rather than quick, or that there are *way* more consequences involved in the veterinary clinic versus simply picking a restaurant for dinner.

To be clear, I am not advocating for careless decision-making in the veterinary hospital, and I understand that an accurate diagnosis on a complex medical case cannot be made in a split second.

However, I implore you to find the right balance between thorough decision-making that's both quick and effective. And you can find this sweet spot by breaking decision-making down.

That brings me to *Doctor of Veterinary Medicine*, or *D.V.M.*, which is actually not what it sounds like! Instead, we're looking at the acronym I've developed for decision-making:

Decide. Verbalize. Move Forward.

As a veterinarian, you are in the service industry. When a client walks through the doors to your clinic with their pet, they have questions and problems that they expect you to answer and alleviate, respectively.

With that in mind, I've found that the best way to keep everyone on the same page while minimizing my indecision fatigue was to always remember that *I am a D.V.M.* I'll walk you through each step.

#1 Decide

One frustration I ran into coming out of university was the idea that I needed to run *all* the tests on every one of my cases! The reality is far different. Doing every single test was usually impractical, a waste of time, and often not an economic option for the client.

It was based in the thought that I had to meet some kind of "gold standard" for the client, where every possible test and treatment was on offer. It made sense at the university clinic, where we became accustomed to the "gold standard" because then we did have every option available to us.

But that doesn't always exist in practice. Once I accepted that the "gold standard" varies with each individual case depending on the client's needs, I was able to tailor the care I gave based on each client's expressed goals.

I then set the target to decide on very clear and actionable next steps that I could employ by the end of each appointment. Is it a vaccine appointment? Great. The pet is healthy, we will give it the vaccines now. Is this a complex medical case? No worries. What is the next most appropriate test that I need to run to land on a definitive diagnosis or rule out differentials? There is *always* a definitive next step that can be taken.

Therefore, instead of exhaustively going through all scenarios and options, I would focus on the most important next step. You can and should still be aware of all the possible avenues a case can take, but you don't want to get caught up with so many options that you end up making no useful decisions at all.

There is an old saying in vet school that goes, *When you hear hoof beats, think horses, not zebras.* This certainly applies here!

#2 Verbalize

Once you've listened to the client's needs and decided on the most important next step, verbalize your verdict.

Communication is key! Think about how your client feels when they're sitting on the other side of the exam table. Depending on the case, they may be terrified thinking about the fate of their beloved pet. Verbalize exactly what you would like to do and exactly why you are doing it. Will this test give you a definitive diagnosis, or will it simply rule out something major? Will they get an answer after this one test, or is likely that this is just the start of a series of tests?

And it's not just about verbalization with the client: excellent written communication on the patient's hospital file is a must! Could someone else pick this file up and know what's going on? This is mandatory if you want to limit needing to repeat this process or being bothered with questions on your day off.

Part of verbalization is also making sure that all the right people are present to hear your communication. How often have you clearly laid out your beautiful treatment plan only to have a significant other walk into the exam room and ask you to repeat everything you just said? It happens all the time! To save time and energy try to have all of the decision-makers present when verbalizing key decisions.

At the end of the day, the more people know what's happening, the better. Remember that *frustration exists in the gap between expectations and reality*. Communication will help limit this gap.

#3 Move Forward

This is the part that can make or break you.

In my experience, the *M* of *D.V.M.* was the area where I would get the most stuck and therefore fatigued. Whether it was due to ruminating on a decision or considering too many options, refusing to move forward really hurt my decision-making process.

In reality, a decision with no action is just a wish or a thought, and if there is no action, you haven't actually made a decision. Make your decisions with conviction, then leave them in the past. The exception here, of course, is being faced with new information—which can and should always lead you to revisit.

I also want to note here that ultimately, the decisions around patients are their owners' responsibility. They will lean on you because you are the expert, but at the end of the day, the tough choices are theirs to make—all we can give them is guidance. We can't carry the weight of everyone's decisions around.

Profound Decisions

Devin was a classmate of mine at the start of veterinary school, but he didn't show up for the second year. I soon found out why: he was one of the few people (and perhaps the only) to survive an airway fire. I learned that he had gone in for surgery to have a polyp removed from his vocal cords. It should have been a quick, in-and-out surgery, but the laser they were using ignited in the presence of pure oxygen. His upper airway caught on fire from the inside.

He woke up in the hospital a few days later after being in a medically induced coma and, surprised to see himself surrounded by his family, was left wondering what had happened. He quickly had to deal with the reality that he had survived a major medical accident—which by all accounts was a miracle—and that he still faced a very long and dangerous road to recovery.

When he was discharged from the hospital and returned home, he went upstairs to his bedroom and sat on the edge of his bed. In that moment, he realized that although his life had profoundly changed and he had been incredibly lucky to have survived, there would still be years of battling to overcome his injuries. And then he decided, right then and there, that he wouldn't give up, that he was going to survive.

He had made a *profound decision*. That's what happens when you stick your stake in the ground and say, *this is my stance. This is what's going to happen.*

And his profound decision became reality. Devin still has to deal with constant check-ups, surgeries, and the lingering effects of the incident, but he survived. He returned to vet school, went on to become a successful clinical veterinarian and veterinary clinic owner, and 15 years later, he told his remarkable story on *The Veterinary Project* podcast.[15]

Profound decisions have little to do with decision fatigue or indecision fatigue. Rather, these are the life-changing decisions that only come up a handful of times in your life.

To illustrate this, if I were to ask you, "What is your name?" you would know the answer with absolute certainty because every cell in your body believes it to be true. Profound decisions are made with this level of conviction. From the moment that definitive decision is made, the course of your life will be forever altered.

Profound decisions have the ability to positively change your life, and opportunities to make them exist all around us and happen at the most random of times.

I believe these big moments can be hard for people to grasp and honor because fear and self-consciousness often take over—I certainly felt that when I realized I wanted to start working part-time. In addition, going down the path you know is right for you may be difficult because of outside influences, being forced to leave a comfort zone, or your life being changed in a significant way.

For these reasons, it takes strength and courage to act on profound decisions. Yes, the consequences of these moments have the potential to be massive (and generally speaking, the bigger the consequences, the harder of a time someone has with the decision) but I urge you to follow through with a profound decision when you are faced with one.

The power lies in each and every one of us to alter the course of our life at any point we desire.

Choices Need to Be Made Everywhere, Every Day

I remember the first time I told someone other than Rosalie that I was going to start working part-time, three days a week, as a vet.

My dad had come to visit me in Saskatoon to help me renovate a new property. As we were painting the walls together, a moment of silence fell between us. I took the opportunity to tell him, "Hey, Dad...I wanted to give you a small life update."

"What's that?" he replied, still moving the foam roller up and down the wall.

"It's about my career. One day, I just realized that I was going to be stuck in this position forever—working these long hours every day, being exhausted when I came home, and never making as much money as I wanted to. So, I put in my two weeks the next day."

"Hm?" He paused halfway up the wall, now giving me his full attention.

"Yep...I'm heading to a new clinic, where I'll be working three days a week."

Switching from working as a full-time vet to part-time was something I had never seriously considered prior to that moment—especially because I didn't have a "socially acceptable" reason to do so. Rosalie and I didn't have kids yet, nor had any other life-changing event happened that would require more of my attention. I just wanted a change. (This was before the point in my evolution where I realized I didn't need permission to make this change. My own desire to do it was *all* that I needed.)

My dad was silent. I watched as he tried to piece everything together in his head so he could understand where I was coming from. But he was a farmer through and through—the traditional idea of "hard work" was engrained into his DNA. This was one of the reasons I respected my dad so much, however, it might have made it hard for him to understand my decision. And he wasn't alone in this. I gathered similar confusion from colleagues, friends, and peers.

Other people's skepticism made it harder to go through with my decision, but I am ultimately glad I did. It changed my life for the better.

As a veterinarian, the stream of decisions that are funneled your way will never end. As Brennen A. McKenzie puts it in a study of clinical decision-making, "Performing surgery and other manual skills and communicating with colleagues and clients are important, but there is nothing we do as often or that is ultimately as central to clinical medicine as making decisions."[16] It's part of our job to make choices quickly and decisively, but it becomes extremely difficult to do so when we grapple with things like decision fatigue and indecision fatigue.

The tactical tips earlier in this chapter will help, but you have to go deeper than that. As discussed, I encourage you to look inside yourself and recognize when indecision is eating at you. Look out for fear-based choices, use the D.V.M. method, and welcome profound decisions when they come your way. After all, the betterment of ourselves, our careers, and the lives of our clients depends on it!

And remember, decisions got you here. You, the person that is reading this book right now, is the exact result of all your previous life decisions, and who you will be five years from now will be exactly the result of all the decisions you make between now and then.

Decisions really do dictate your life.

Chapter Five

Empathy Alchemy

YOU MET MISERABLE Mike a few chapters ago. Realizing I was him was my rock bottom, but issues with capacity weren't the only thing that got me to that place. When I look back at Miserable Mike now, I can clearly see what ingredients made him. It went something like this...

- A dollop of capacity overload

- A dash of decision and indecision fatigue

- A pinch of perfectionism

- A sprinkle of empathy fatigue

I know they aren't the most specific measurements, but you get the point. Miserable Mike was born from a combination of these things. In this chapter, we're going to talk about one contributor in particular: *empathy fatigue.*

Empathy fatigue is essentially the diminishing of one's ability to understand and share the feelings of others after extended periods of doing so. It's not binary like a broken arm where either your arm is broken or not. Empathy fatigue can exist on a spectrum, and it has many different possible presentations and symptoms. In other words, it may look different on you than on me. That means it could be affecting you in ways you don't even realize.

Despite how it may sound at this point, empathy is actually a good thing. Tania Singer and Olga M. Klimecki highlight this in "Empathy and Compassion," stating that empathy is the "general capacity to resonate with other's emotional states."[17] As humans, we are social creatures—and nothing is more exemplary of this than when we veterinarians meet with a client in the exam room. In order for the client to trust us, we have to use and display empathy because this develops rapport and builds trust. Empathy is very powerful, so don't be afraid to use it in appropriate dosages!

Empathy in Reality

Almost every time I listen to the frustrations of an experienced veterinarian, some version of empathy fatigue is high on their list—and it's easy to imagine why! After years of working in high stress and vast emotional situations, a degree of fatigue is bound to creep in.

It can be exhausting to exist in an environment where we are expected to constantly have and display an immense amount of empathy, even though we don't always receive it back. In this chapter, we will tackle:

- Dealing with clients that lack empathy

- Having to maintain high levels of empathy

I would love to tell you that (in mere paragraphs!) you will unpack the cure for one of the most exhausting aspects of veterinary medicine, but that is unfortunately not the case. The solution lies in learning how to avoid empathetic distress while accepting that empathy and compassion will always be critical in the veterinary profession.

It's essential that we address these problems to protect ourselves from overuse and abuse of empathy. However, it will come down to us continually doing the work to recognize when our empathy is running low or slipping into distress, to learn how to conserve it, and recharge when we can.

Let's unpack!

Unexpected Exhaustion

Sometimes, the most fatiguing cases are the ones you don't see coming.

It's pretty obvious that you're about to be hit with a major case and the heightened emotions that come with it when an emergency comes flying through the door of the clinic, like when a client's dog is hit by a car. They crash through the front door screaming, carrying their limp dog in their arms like a baby.

Every other client in the waiting room perks up and can immediately feel the panic and anxiety. The client, oblivious to the fact that they are covered in blood, temporarily leaves the whole room breathless.

It's pure chaos, and you know you're going to be on an emotional rollercoaster until it's resolved. These situations are not uncommon in a veterinary clinic, and no doubt they're challenging ones to navigate.

But you're aware of what you're getting into in emergency cases like these—you're prepared for them and can navigate them accordingly.

What catches you off guard is what happens *after* you resolve the emergency and move on to the next appointment on your schedule. You're now very, very late to it and the client is furious.

So, after changing out of blood-stained clothes, you head into your scheduled vaccine appointment and are confronted by an angry client who has been waiting for over an hour. They unleash all their frustration onto you with a fury. A fury you did not see coming. A fury that leaves you emotionally bruised and scarred.

This is what I like to call *unexpected empathetic exhaustion.*

You knew the emergency case was going to drain you, but there was no way you could've foreseen the sweet puppy's vaccine appointment going this way—all due to some client's lack of understanding. It blindsides you.

You would expect them to have a little more empathy for you considering they too witnessed the trail of blood that led to the back of the clinic. And when you don't get that, it can be hard to process—particularly because you've been consistently giving empathy to them.

But the reality is this. Everyone perceives things differently, so it doesn't matter whether the situation is dire or just perceived to be dire. If it's real to the client, then it's real. There could be other things going on in the client's life—maybe they're late for another appointment because of this one. All of this provides some context and understanding, but it doesn't excuse bad behavior.

Simply put, we as veterinarians have a very well-developed toolbox full of ways to navigate difficult emotional situations, but not everyone has these skills.

In discussions about this very issue, colleagues, friends, and I dove into the idea of training people how to treat us, which brought me to the conclusion that *we often get what we tolerate.*

Learning to draw the line somewhere is necessary for your emotional well-being, your staff's emotional well-being, and the overall functioning of the clinic. These things must take priority over accommodating the lack of emotional control of a few clients or colleagues.

In our profession, even though we do not have 100% control over the relationships we have with clients (anyone can walk through the door), we do have control over who we allow to return and eliminating the most toxic ones.

I believe that our industry has done a poor job of tolerating abusive behavior from clients because we're encouraged to think that "the client is always right" or "it's all about the pets" until it gets to the point where we sacrifice ourselves as martyrs to abusive clients in the name of caring for their pets. However, there's an enormous benefit to firing clients because it allows us to regain freedom over our professional relationships. That means you need to:

1. Face these clients head on. Tell them their behavior will not be tolerated, and that they can either adjust or leave.

2. If the client refuses to adjust, don't be afraid to fire them.

In my clinical experience, the clients that require this kind of treatment are in the vast minority, a tiny fraction of the rest. But as Pareto's Principle, or the 80/20 Rule, theorizes, something small can have a big effect on you. What that means for you is that 80% of your emotional stress in the vet clinic can come from the behavior of only 20% of your clients.

(In my experience, I would argue that only 1% of my clients were troublesome, but they still were the cause of greater than 80% of my emotional stress. To be clear, this 1% were being unreasonable over minor things or just being outright assholes, which is very different from a highly emotional client during traumatic appointments.)

This slight percentage of clients, however, is breaking veterinarians. The profession must work both collectively and individually toward a solution. Once the profession, clinics, and individual veterinary professionals take a firm stance and state that they will no longer tolerate this type of behavior—that they are not door mats—everyone will be able to move forward collectively to elevate the veterinary profession.

We need to save our emotional energy for what it was meant for: caring for our deserving clients and their pets!

It's time to internalize that the customer is *not* always right, just as no person can be.

We've talked about the small percentage of clients that are extremely fatiguing in their own right. We're now going to look at more day-to-day empathy fatigue caused by high levels of empathy output and when empathy slips into empathetic distress.

High-Empathy Output

Veterinarians pour out empathy every day, constantly connecting to the emotional states of our clients. To alleviate the high-empathy output problem, I will share two perspective shifts that helped me navigate the sheer volume of empathy I found myself delivering on a daily basis.

Changing your perspective will not give you an infinite supply of empathy, but it will help you be more compassionate.

Listen. Listen. Listen.

One of the things I struggled with early on in my career was the notion that I needed to have an answer for everything—a thought that makes sense considering our background. We're constantly required to provide concrete responses to whatever is being thrown at us. Answer these questions on this test. Diagnose these symptoms. Come up with a treatment plan. And so it goes on.

For example, during a euthanasia, while everyone was gently petting and comforting their beloved pet as it took its last breaths, I would feel the need to say something profound. I felt like I had to neatly package the emotions my clients were feeling—as if it was my responsibility to bestow something deeply meaningful onto them because I was the vet.

But the problem was exactly that: I was just a vet. I could recite an encyclopedia of veterinarian medicine knowledge to them, but my specialty was not in the greater meaning of life.

My mistake early on was providing this "wisdom" to them because I was uncomfortable in the silence, and I wanted that feeling to stop. But that was not what the client was looking for.

It didn't take long to learn that clients in difficult situations just wanted a vet's compassion and to be heard. From that moment on, I focused on giving them my full attention and simply being present with them as they navigated the circumstance they were in.

Suddenly, euthanasia appointments became sessions where the client would recount all the most wonderful memories they had of their pet. A journey through the pet's life as the owner came to terms with its ending. And when the owner's gaze eventually fell on me, as it always did, I would offer a smile or kind word about how great a companion their pet had been. Often, this would result in everyone sitting in silence for several minutes just being present.

Once I understood that clients just wanted me to listen and be there with them, this silence was no longer uncomfortable. That's why talking less and listening more is the key.

There is a saying that goes, *We have two ears and one mouth so that we can listen twice as much as we speak.* There is a great deal of truth to this, but I'd argue that this ratio isn't nearly high enough.

Everyone is going through something.

Empathy was always easier for me to practice during a euthanasia because the emotions of the appointment didn't catch me off guard.

As veterinarians, we begin preparing for it the moment we see the typical euthanasia color block on our schedule. We expect that this will be an emotional appointment in either direction—oftentimes the client is sad and mourns, sometimes they're joyous and celebrate life. Either way, we know there will be an elevated state of emotion.

But it's much more challenging to practice empathy when this preparation is absent. You'll easily be thrown off if you're expecting to walk into a routine vaccination appointment, but are bombarded with crying, anger, or verbal abuse.

Therefore, the second perspective-shift I ask you to adopt is to constantly remember that everyone is going through something. Internalizing this belief will unfortunately not get rid of empathy fatigue, but it will make it much easier to manage it.

Take for instance finding a "lump" on a pet during a routine vaccination. You and I both know there are a countless number of things this lump could be, but the second we mention the word "lump" to the client, they're going to jump to "cancer." All the negative feelings that come with that word will rise to the surface and implode on *you*.

Whenever this would happen, I would often get thrown off by their strong reaction, but when I shifted my perspective and started making no assumptions about the person standing across from me, it become less taxing on me. Instead of thinking, *Wow, that person really overreacted to a lipoma*, I'd return to the thought that I know nothing about their situation. Cancer could be a specific trigger for them—maybe a loved one has it, they've lost someone to it, or they have it themselves. You never know.

I would then revert to the idea that they're simply facing a gap in expectations and reality, a gap that only I could close as their medical professional. Like magic, the emotions would instantly settle.

Even when I didn't know what was triggering a client's emotional response—such as when I'd walk into the room for a routine appointment and a client was already emotional—I was better able to manage my response to them by reserving judgment and instead focusing on wishing them well.

Empathetic Distress

During the majority of my veterinarian career, I had a cat named Preid. When he was a middle-aged cat, around six or seven years old, he got really sick—and I mean all of it. He was losing weight, vomiting, having diarrhea, and losing muscle mass. I ran every test I could think of, but nothing definitive came back. I put him on some trial medications, but none of them helped. I even took him in to see specialists at the nearest university, but no one could figure out what was wrong with him.

Having endured all the stress that came from my personal cat's case, I'm sure you can imagine what happened to me whenever a cat with a similar signalment came in to see me at work. I would connect *deeply* to the client and their pet during that first appointment, feeling every wave of emotion that they did. In other words, I would experience high-empathy output.

Things started to deteriorate as the case became chronic, when clients saw me multiple times and received multiple inconclusive tests. These kinds of cases would drag on for months—because the clients loved their cat so much, just like I did, they were willing to do whatever it took.

High-empathy output becomes a problem here because over time, the case becomes personal. *Empathetic distress* is what happens when you *take on* the pain of the client and mix in your own pet's story with theirs.

When you slip into empathetic distress, you will experience a strong, adverse reaction to the suffering of someone else, which helps no one. Unlike having deep compassion for a person (where you feel "for" them), you enter a state of feeling "with" them that becomes *too* strong. Eventually, your past experiences will mix with the client's current experiences until your focus becomes protecting yourself from the pain you're going through in the present. You might withdraw or pull away at first, but left unchecked, empathetic distress will lead to full on burnout.

This is the super fatiguing part of empathy fatigue, which is why you need to learn to rely on compassion instead.

Compassion DOES NOT Fatigue

Beyond my anecdotal experience in the clinic, research is beginning to provide us with some insight and functional paths forward. For most of my clinical veterinary career, compassion fatigue and empathy fatigue were used interchangeably, but as Dr. Trisha Dowling points out, "Compassion does not fatigue!"[18]

Neurobiologically speaking, acts of empathy and acts of compassion activate very different parts of our brain and produce very different results. While empathy can trigger pain networks that deplete dopamine, compassion actually triggers reward centers and is neurologically rejuvenating.

If that's true, how can we begin to turn empathy into compassion? Dowling suggests mindfulness-based meditation, stating, "The most well-studied techniques for compassion skills are found in mindfulness meditation programs. Even with short periods of compassion training, participants continue to feel empathy for the suffering of others, but gain the capacity to feel positive emotions without feeling distress."[19]

The shift comes from the fact that empathetic distress comes from "feeling with," but to the point that you are unable to distinguish the pain of others from your own, whereas compassion is "feeling for," or recognizing the pain but not owning it. Mindfulness works in tandem with this idea because it helps build the skill of experiencing and noticing events while being present, without focusing the emotions on ourselves. I have found that mindfulness helps me slow down and be present with my clients without experiencing distress.

My own personal experience with mindfulness meditation has been exceptionally challenging but infinitely rewarding. I often rediscover just how many squirrels are running around in my head. Over the years I have modified my mindfulness practice to what works for me, and sometimes it is something as simple as a walk through the park just to notice the clouds. I can confidently say it has been one of the most useful skills I have added to my toolbox (more on this later).

Empathy Expert

One thing we have yet to talk about in this chapter is the fact that not all of your empathy fatigue necessarily comes from clients. Colleagues can also contribute to the problem, especially if you're working in a toxic environment. While these interpersonal issues are typically too unique for general advice, I will say that compassion is a tool that can be used in the workplace to better it for yourself and others.

I have seen some beautiful relationships form between colleagues inside of the clinic, and have experienced some of them myself. Because the work we all do is so hard and can even be traumatizing at times, it's pretty incredible that we can recognize when a colleague is slipping into empathetic distress and help them through it. Compassion, in these cases, can be used outwardly and not just internally.

Overall, empathy is a very important part of our profession.

In fact, it's very likely a large part of what got you into veterinarian medicine in the first place: you care. And yet, continually experiencing empathetic distress can lead to burnout, so it is critical that veterinarians learn how to navigate empathy.

With simple tools such as listening, shifting perspective, and practicing mindfulness, my hope is that you can reach a place where you're able to experience empathy alchemy.

Chapter Six

The Right Thing Isn't Always Easy

MORALLY DISTRESSING SITUATIONS are something most vets will encounter at one point or another. In my opinion, it's one of the least talked about but incredibly fatiguing aspects of veterinary medicine—and the data backs that up. A survey taken by North American veterinarians found that "73% of respondents stated that not being able to do the right thing for a patient caused their staff moderate to severe stress and 78% replied that it caused them moderate to severe distress."[20] Furthermore, "62% said that they sometimes or often felt that clients put them in a no-win situation where they couldn't 'do the right thing.'"[21] But moral distress can be less in-your-face than these circumstances—it can be subtle, such as when you are unable to provide care to a patient because the owner cannot afford it. It can also happen inside the clinic, when you and a colleague disagree on something or when they practice something you don't stand for.

Because we see the entire spectrum of the human population, it's not surprising that we will encounter people with different views and beliefs from our own. Most of the time, this is not a problem—it's the nature of being human.

But when you encounter clients who are on the extreme ends of any spectrum, something else happens. You're left speechless, confused, and, potentially, in moral distress. For veterinarians, these events can occur in a variety of ways. Sometimes it's when someone asks you to perform a medical procedure that goes against your personal core values or is unethical. Maybe it's after some verbal insinuations. Or maybe it's not after an interaction with a client at all; vet-to-vet disagreements, bullying, discrimination, and microaggressions can cause moral distress as well.

Any outsider would be shocked to discover the astounding things heard in a veterinarian clinic. I've heard clients ramble about every way possible they can "euthanize" their pet after questioning doing it at the clinic. I've listened to owners complain about the expensive nature of anesthetics and pain killers and eventually proclaim that I could *and should* do a surgery without them. And I've been told over and over again that I am forcing a client to murder their pet.

In some circumstances, a case becomes full-on psychological warfare—and you're always stuck right in the middle of it.

This leaves you to grapple with the aching effects of moral distress. One scenario in which it can play out is something like this. You know that what the client wants to happen is morally distressing for you. You also know that they will continue to search for and eventually find a veterinarian who will do what they're requesting, no questions asked. On the other hand, you just want what is best for the pet and know that you may be their only option for fair, painless treatment. What on Earth are you supposed to do?

This is a very gray, anxiety-inducing area to sit in, and—worst of all—this instance might not be the only morally distressing dilemma you're dealing with at the time. There could be one, two, or even 10 other issues going on at once!

These sorts of dilemmas certainly took their toll on me in my early career.

Looking back, this was partially because I lacked the confidence to deny the "customer is always right" paradigm. The frequency in which I was asked to do these things also played a role in my moral distress, but the greatest stressor was that I was simply unprepared for and unequipped to deal with these situations when I was starting out. I never anticipated that I would form such adversarial relationships with a few clients.

Veterinary medical associations can help with such situations, which is why they're so important. For example, I have always personally been against ear cropping (which is, as you may already know, a cosmetic surgical procedure that involves cutting and shaping the floppy portion of a dog's ear so that it stands up), but saying "No" was never an issue for me because our local veterinary medical association banned it. Therefore, I could just lean on their regulations when I lacked the confidence or courage to do it myself.

But these regulations aren't always there for you to rely on.

The truth of the matter is that the service we provide involves caring for an actual living and breathing being—so we have to take a stand. So, let's discuss how you can do just that while also retaining your professionalism, keeping your emotional distance from clients, and learning how to manage moral distress.

When They Put the Blame on You

It was just another day in the clinic.

After finishing a routine check-up, I met with a client who

wanted their cat declawed. Not only do I dislike the procedure—it's like cutting the tips off of your fingers—many veterinary medical associations find the practice inhumane and are fighting to ban it. In fact, my local veterinary medical association finally banned cat declaws in September of 2021—but this story took place long before that.

At this point in time at our clinic we had so many clients request, and sometimes demand, this surgery that we were forced to confront it again and again. Every time, I would try to direct the client to alternative options first, like soft paws or behavior discussion. But oftentimes, the client would still want the procedure done and proclaim that they were just going to find a place that would do it if we wouldn't.

And so, I would be left with a terrible decision: Do I perform a procedure I don't believe in because I'll be able to prescribe aggressive pain medication to help the cat handle it? Or do I let the client go somewhere else, where the cat's pain may not even be managed or the procedure would be done at a lower standard? (I had been consulted on enough of these "lower standard" post-operative rechecks to realize this was a real concern.)

At first, I took the stance in clinic that I would perform the procedure (with all proper pain medication) *only* after the client gave non-surgical options a try. If the client refused to try non-surgical options, they would have to go elsewhere, leaving me wondering about the outcome. When they at least tried other options but still demanded the procedure, I would go through with it, managing the cat's pain as best as I could, but would also feel terrible that I had taken away a portion of the cat's natural behavior.

Eventually, I got to the point where I would no longer do the surgery. The line just needed to be drawn and I felt it was the right thing to do. So, on that day, I explained our stance to the client.

"What do you mean you can't do it?"

"I'm sorry, but we don't perform that surgery here. I would be happy to discuss alternatives with you."

The client went silent, their face wore a look of shock.

What always stood out to me about that moment was the fact that I stopped trying to convince the client to do otherwise, manage them, or control the outcome at my expense. I also didn't leave any room for discussion. Instead, I accepted that I had to live by my standards but could not force others to do the same.

This brings me to my first piece of advice:

1. **Learn to say "No."**

When it comes to moral distress, you need to acquire the skill of limiting it. You do this by creating boundaries for yourself and others, because, ultimately, you're the one who has to live with the decision you made. Not the client. Not another person in the clinic. *You.* You can't control all outcomes, but you can live according to your own moral compass.

In the situation above, while it's true that the owner may take their pet somewhere else that doesn't provide the same level of care that we would, at least I know I took a stand for what I believed in.

At the end of the day, the more you run your practice by your own standards, the more you will find clients that align with them—which will ultimately create a better and less morally distressing working environment for you. Morally distressing situations will continue to pop up, but boundaries help to slowly eliminate the repeat offenders.

In the grand scheme of things, I will admit that cat declaws were pretty low on my moral distress scale. Being confronted with requests such as euthanizing healthy pets or hearing tales of surgeries performed with a rubber boot as an anesthetic machine always made me cringe.

No matter what was causing the moral distress, the one thing I could rely on was pet owners transferring blame onto me, especially when they had a financial constraint.

Let's say, for example, that someone brings in a cat who cannot urinate, which is a very common problem for male cats. Unfortunately, it is often a life-or-death decision for owners.

There are really only three options: fix the problem, euthanize the cat, or allow the cat to suffer in agony until it eventually passes away. The first two options leave the owner with a substantial veterinary bill and the third wasn't an option to me.

That's when I would get hit with comments like, "You are going to make me kill my pet," or, "I'm just going to take him home and shoot him."

I have compassion for people in these situations because they didn't come into the clinic expecting to have to make a life-or-death decision, nor did they foresee being put in this type of financial position. More often than not, they thought the problem was going to be a quick, minor fix, so now they're in an emotionally heightened situation where they feel helpless and lost—which causes them to take it out on the nearest person.

But that doesn't change the fact that the nearest person is us and our staff.

I have worked in both rural areas and cities. The dollar amounts may differ, but the situation in which pet owners shift the blame onto the veterinarian does not. Thus, the second piece of advice I have to offer is what my first veterinary mentor told me:

2. It's their problem, not yours.

When clients are trying to make the problem your fault, try to remember you are there to provide solutions and help in any way you can, but your job description does not include carrying around a client's responsibilities. Sometimes things get to a point where you have to set a boundary. Ultimately, every issue is the pet owner's issue. We just physically and emotionally can't carry them all.

This isn't to say that we should be cavalier about our cases, but we should embrace the fact there is a certain lack of control in this profession—and there is something freeing about that. We cannot force someone to do something, nor can we change everything we do to accommodate them. Because if we did, we would spiral into empathetic distress, which, as we know, results in empathy fatigue and burnout. And, as we discussed last chapter, we really should be coming from a place of compassion, not empathy overload.

This is a perfect segue to powerful words by Les Brown:

3. "If you do what is easy, your life will be hard. But if you do what is hard, your life will be easy."

I find this quote very applicable to moral distress.

For the veterinarian, having these difficult conversations once means that, overall, your career will be easier because you will have already dealt with an issue and know the best way to solve it for next time, instead of just kicking the can down the road. And in doing so, you are also *teaching your clients how to treat you.*

If you ignore a morally distressing situation and never have the courage to have that difficult conversation, you are simply inviting more of the same into your life. For instance, if a client figures out they can ask for whatever, whenever they want, no matter how unethical, they will never stop taking advantage of you. That's why you need to either eliminate these types of clients from your practice or correct their behavior before it becomes a recurring problem.

Take a stand. Set the right tone for the relationship from the beginning.

This is also applicable to discrimination in the vet clinic. One example of this is the offensive names clients sometimes give to their pets. We can't control or change what a client is going to call their pet, but we can control whether or not their pet will receive care from you. This is an instance where you should take a stand because if you don't, you will find yourself grappling with moral distress every time you see the pet or have to say their name. Deal with it right away so it's not a lingering issue.

Consequently, with any aspect of moral distress, the ultimate solution is not to run away from it, but step toward it. This brings me to my next recommendation:

4. **You're 100% responsible for your happiness.**

As you know by now, this is one of my core tenets.

It took me a long time to realize it, but my emotional state was 100% my own doing.

If we were to go back in time, I would have argued you to death that it was entirely the opposite—that I had no control over my situation, that I felt a particular way because of an external reason. Something or someone was always at fault, but it was never me.

Ironically, clients would blame me for everything under the sun, but I was blaming all of my unhappiness on everything *but* me.

When I look back on my mental state, I'm now able to see that I was defining myself as a victim. I'm not sure how I reached the point where I felt like a victim, and I'll talk more about it in the upcoming chapter on identity, but I know one thing for certain: nothing else you do to work on yourself matters if you trap yourself in a victim mentality.

Just like it's your clients' responsibility to make their own decisions, it's yours to take care of yourself. Having support from others can help, but no one else can change your outlook besides you.

There will always be bad days. There will always be things that go wrong. And there will always be an excuse to not be happy.

But you can define that for yourself. While we cannot control the words or actions of others, we can work on controlling how we respond to them and setting appropriate boundaries.

Lastly, the most important advice of all:

5. Define your core values.

To be courageous enough to do everything we've talked about so far, you first need to clearly define what your personal core values are.

Think of your core values as your north star, a light that will guide you in the metaphorical darkness. If you don't define them and embody them in advance of taking action or making a decision in a particular situation, you will be too easily swayed or just not know where you are going. When we are under stress (as you would be in a morally distressing situation), we can only perform to the level of our preparation so we must, therefore, have done the work on our core values in advance.

To determine your core values, ask yourself, "What do I, as a person, actually stand for?" Defining your core values is a considerable exercise. I encourage you to dedicate significant thought and time on this.

Dr. John Demartini is someone I have followed for years. I consider him to be one of the foremost experts on helping people to determine their values and live in alignment with those values to get the most out of life. I recommend you do his "Value Determination Process" quiz online—a great tool to help you discover what your values are.[22]

I want to mention a tendency I have noticed in regard to working on your core values. People commonly write down what they *think* they should write down (e.g. *Be a hard worker, be authentic*, etc.). While I believe there is merit in these kinds of core values, I also want to urge you to make specific and memorable ones. As Trevor Throness astutely said on an episode of *The Veterinary Project* podcast, "It's not what's written on the walls, it's what happens in the halls."[23] You don't want your core values to be beautiful little sentiments that you hang up on a wall and forget about later—you want them to be ingrained into how you live and to represent uniquely *you*. If your actions don't represent your core values, then you are not being honest about who you are.

Accept that your core values will change over time—and that is OK. This doesn't mean you should adopt a "set it and forget it" mindset with your core values. Instead, treat them as a living document that you continue to revisit and adapt as you evolve.

Finally, core values are invaluable for a multitude of reasons, but one of them goes back to Chapter 4: decision-making. When your core values are crystal clear and true to you, they help you to make definitive decisions and stick to them.

Knowing what your core values are at the drop of a hat will help you in emotionally heightened situations. Instead of showing any trace of hesitance, you'll be able to instantly act according to your personal standards. That shows everyone that you know who you are and what you stand for.

Microchip Morality

Early in my career, a client brought in a pit bull that had bitten someone. They wanted me to make the problem go away by removing its microchip and putting in a new one so the dog couldn't be identified as the biter and subsequently euthanized.

This case was clearly outside my ethical boundaries—there was no way I was going to go through with it. But that didn't mean they didn't put pressure on me. I had to say "No" multiple times on many different occasions, even when this client—who was considerably larger than me—saw me at the gym.

You will get no warning that these types of clients are coming in, so to be prepared for them, you need to build up the skills we've talked about in this book and be clear in advance about what your core values are.

Ultimately, moral distress in the veterinarian profession is never going to completely go away. There will always be patients that we can't care for in the way we would like, unethical clients, and, unfortunately, those that just operate under a completely different moral code. We can't completely control these things, but we can control how we respond to them—and we do that by leaning into our core values and continuously expanding our tactical skillset.

Chapter Seven

I Am

I CAN'T PINPOINT THE exact year, certainly not the exact day—
and truthfully, I wasn't even aware of it in the moment—but
somewhere around year seven or eight into my career, I stopped
growing professionally.

Pretty much anything that could walk (or not walk) through
the clinic door (including emergencies) became routine to me. And
if it wasn't routine, I encouraged cases to flow to specialists rather
than tackle them myself. I became complacent in not adding any
new tools or skills to my repertoire.

Looking back, I realize I was functioning well within my comfort zone because I'd lost the drive to grow within my role. In
turn, my passion for my career further diminished as my daily case
load grew increasingly mundane. Work was becoming noticeably
less engaging, purposeful, and fulfilling—even though it was ever
more stressful and fatiguing.

Now, imagine identity like a pie chart. I have often found—
and have personally felt—that a veterinarian's pie chart is largely
made up of one thing only, where their job title takes up the ma-

jority of their identity. It completely defines them.

Initially, I held on to my identity as a vet very tightly. Any time I met someone new, the first thing that would come out of my mouth after my name was, "I'm a veterinarian." But as my career progressed, I started leaving this out of my introductions. I didn't even like my clients calling me "Doctor" in the exam room. My identity pie chart became more balanced as I became less emotionally attached to my job title. I stopped defining myself only as a veterinarian.

I'm sure some of that comes with age, but I believe I was mostly experiencing an identity crisis. Sure, I was and still am proud of my accomplishments in the veterinary profession, but to be honest, it kind of annoyed me that I was labelled in *just* that capacity. It was rather limiting in many ways.

I had so many other interests I wanted to pursue, such as real estate investing. Saying "I am a veterinarian" when introducing myself became insufficient in capturing that.

In retrospect, I think this change happened because I had spent so many years crafting this meticulous *I am* statement around being a veterinarian that I had never truly given myself permission to be anything else.

And I don't think I'm the only one. A major concern I see in our industry is too many people becoming absolutely entangled in the identity they've created around being a veterinarian.

The Problem with "I Am a Veterinarian"

When one's identity is solely based on being a veterinarian, their self-worth and satisfaction is derived from the external validation of their career by others, and their perceived success in it. Sometimes, a person can even lose focus of other important parts in their life when their perspective is so singular.

Yes, a career is important and you may even consider it your life's work.

However, while I'll agree that it certainly makes up a portion of who you are, I've witnessed self-destruction in the pursuit of external validation far too often.

Personally, I found that the external appearance of my actions was often applauded and admired. *I* was a hard worker. *I* was clinically competent. *I* had strong people skills. *I* had a solid and growing following of clients. By all accounts, I was a high performer, which can be great.

However, if you're performing for all the wrong reasons, things can go off the rails.

So many negative internal beliefs were driving my high performance. For example, if I saw more patients and produced more revenue for the clinic, more people would like me and my income would rise. I eventually thought that if more people liked me and I earned more money, I was worth more as a person. I couldn't even refuse to come in on a day off because I believed that was something only a lazy person would do.

If you're anything like I was, you may be addicted to receiving external validation.

This can become a slippery slope over the long term. Like any emotional response, a person needs to receive more and more stimulus to elicit the desired result over time, meaning that they crave more and more validation. More and more coming in to work on days off.

The real danger here is that the person will eventually do anything to protect their most-prized possession: their identity as a veterinarian. I have witnessed this in our profession time and time again. When someone's personal identity is consumed by the fact that they are a vet, any discussion of the challenges of the profession can feel like a direct personal attack to them.

Again, I'm not presuming everyone has this problem, but I do feel that I'm not alone. For those out there that are indeed absolutely engrossed in the identity of being a veterinarian, I often have two thoughts:

1. They eat, breathe, and sleep all things veterinary medicine. This makes them happy, provides them with purpose, and fulfils them.

2. There are some massive emotional gaps in their lives that they are completely burying under the identity of being a veterinarian.

Obviously, it isn't that black and white—an entire spectrum certainly exists—but I know I was firmly in category 2 for a good portion of my career.

Those closer to category 2 may relate to loving and even craving the emotional feeling that simply mentioning being a veterinarian provides them. Personally, I desperately wanted to be liked by everyone, to feel accepted and valued. After all, at the start of my veterinary education, every single time that I would mention my potential career path to others, I was met with thundering approval.

When I reflect on this, I honestly can't remember a single time that someone reacted negatively to me mentioning my plan to become a veterinarian. Without fail the person across from me would light up with a huge beaming smile and say, "Good for you!" and I would get the dopamine hit I was looking for.

But this is where my emotional gaps became clear.

This was all playing out at a time in my life when I was desperately seeking approval; I was trying to please my parents, assume my sister Jill's role in the family following her accident, and reassure myself that I was on the right path.

And when I started calling myself a veterinarian, all of those things instantly came true. I had people's approval. Everyone liked and accepted me. My parents were proud.

If you're questioning whether or not you relate, I encourage you to investigate the driving forces behind your behavior. The next step to take after this introspection is to talk to the people in your support network and other trusted professionals to gather their perspective. I eventually hired a personal coach, joined mastermind groups, and had one-on-ones with certified therapists.

That being said, know that there is no one-size-fits-all solution to overcoming these tendencies. However, one thing remains true: recognizing them is the only way to start changing them.

If the quality of our life is determined by the quality of the questions we ask, a fitting one in this situation comes from Philip McKernan: "What is your work allowing you to avoid?"

I Am

After realizing that I didn't entirely align with the exclusively veterinarian identity, my journey to uncovering what was more in alignment with me began. And it all started with the statement: *I am.*

This little phrase has the power to be the most constructive or destructive force in our lives.

As the legendary author Brian Tracy once said, "You become what you think about most of the time."[24] It's one of those sentiments that deserves a pause, and it's also the reason why *I am* statements are so important. If you have a penchant for highlighters like I know most vet students circa 2008 did, now would be a good time to break one out.

The important thing to realize about this exercise is that it doesn't matter whether what you tell yourself is true or false. On a subconscious level, our internal emotional self has no ability to distinguish between true or false—it's always treated as true. Furthermore, you are *always* listening. This is why what you say to yourself *matters*.

Now let's look beyond the external "I am a veterinarian" statement you've likely been telling others. What *I am* statements are you telling *yourself*, in the secrecy of your own head? Think of this question as a way to shine a spotlight on any negative self-talk and beliefs that you hold on to. Things like: *I am dumb. I am stupid. I am fat. I am not enough.*

Once these *I am* statements slip past the guard of our conscious mind, they are slowly programmed into our belief system and begin to control our actions. As you can see, you truly do become what you spend most of your time thinking about.

The goal here is to shift awareness to your thoughts and deconstruct them. Maybe you'll discover things you didn't even realize you were saying to yourself. Then, when reflecting on this dialogue and whether it portrays a belief or a lack of belief in yourself, I invite you to ask the following questions: *Is this serving me? Do I want to change it?*

One way to go through this process is by working backwards: inspect *results*, which are caused by *actions*, which are caused by *feelings*, which are caused by *thoughts*.

For example, imagine someone's health isn't where they want it to be (the result). After recognizing that, they analyze their eating habits and notice they are consistently eating very unhealthy lunches at the clinic (the action), which could be driven by any number of feelings. Maybe they feel guilty about taking a proper lunch break because there are so many cases to tackle, or maybe they feel that they are lazy if they take time during the day to eat a nutritious meal (the feeling). Their *I am* statements (thoughts) may look something like: *I am lazy. I am not a team player.*

To re-wire this, they will have to work the other way around and shift their thinking to something that serves them. New thoughts lead to new feelings, which lead to new actions, which lead to new results. Their new *I am* statements may look something like *I am healthy; I am vibrant; I am powerful. I am a team player.* The point is the feelings created by these new *I am* statements should manifest in the new action, namely, actually taking the time to eat that healthy, nutritious lunch. Eventually, the results of improved health will follow. These *I am* statements that serve you need be the default setting that we tell ourselves.

When you pay attention to this internal dialogue, you can pick up on clues that will lead you to areas where you need to dig deeper. Often, however, we do *not* want to look into those areas because they are uncomfortable and painful. In the pursuit of growth, however, this is exactly where we should be looking.

Another quote I love comes from life coach, Rock Thomas: "The words that follow *I am,* follow you."[25] Over time, this has become a mantra of mine—a reminder that your internal self is always listening, so you need to choose the words that follow *I am* carefully.

The Power of the I Am Statement

We've talked a lot about *I am* statements that do not serve you, but we're now going to look at how you can work with them to transform yourself. In addition to highlighting your inner dialogue and self-image, the *I am* statement can be immensely powerful.

Telling yourself such things as *I am strong, I am healthy,* or *I am a great husband/wife/father/mother* can move your thoughts into action.

With repetition, belief, and conviction, these *I am* statements become more of a reality for you. Remember, your subconscious believes whatever it is told. Of course, it isn't as simple as standing in front of mirror shouting at yourself all day... In fact, it works nothing like this. If you repeat *I am rich* to yourself a million times you're not just magically going to become rich. A compelling *I am* statement must move you into action.

One thing that makes this easier is language. Keep in mind that everything you need to grow and evolve is already within you—which means you can shift your language around your goals to reflect that. For example, try to avoid talking about your goals with *I want* statements. Want is a weak word. It implies you don't already have access to the thing you're seeking. It implies the results lay somewhere outside of you. *Commit* is a much more powerful word. *I commit* statements imply that you already have everything you need to accomplish them.

For example, *I want to be healthy* seems more like a wish and far more out of reach than *I commit to being healthy.* Committing is a definitive statement.

That brings me to the most powerful tool at your disposal for creating your identity: you.

You get to decide on each and every *I am* statement that passes between your ears. Eliminate those that do not serve you and choose the ones you keep carefully.

You become what you think about, most of the time.

I Am Michael

Only after I recognized the wild loop I was on—where my subconscious thoughts were dictating my actions and producing more of the results I didn't want—was I able to break the cycle.

After my destructive *I am* thoughts were replaced by *I am* statements that served me, I uncovered my true identity.

I am Michael. And that is enough.

At the end of the day, we don't need to be defined by anything external at all—even your name is just a word—so you can make your *I am* statement whatever you want. Whatever you decide, whether it be one or many things, take out a pen and write your new *I am* statement(s) below. This is just the beginning of the work we're going to do on *your internal environment* (more on this later).

Chapter Eight

The Ball Is in Your Court

I N CHAPTER 7, we talked about shifting the way you see yourself. Great—now what? You can't just write some words down on a piece of paper and hope your new ideology sticks. If you want a more permanent change, you need to do the work, specifically in your subconscious, so let's get into it.

By the time you're an adult, *the majority of your thoughts come from your subconscious mind.* This is important to know.

I think we often know this intellectually, but we don't truly grasp it. We *think* we are making our own choices, but really we only actively decide a fraction of what we do in a day. The vast majority of our life happens on auto-pilot—about 95%, actually.[26]

It's like driving a car. After years of experience, you typically don't even realize that you turned the key, buckled your seat belt, and began driving. Your subconscious mind took over. Blocks later something startles you and you realize that you don't remember the last five minutes of driving.

This can play out in your veterinary career as well. After enough years of experience, most things seem routine—it's easy to not be present. Think back to the last time you took a patient's temperature and second guessed whether you actually did so or not; or think about the times you have listened to a patient's heart rate and rhythm and then questioned whether there were abnormalities or not. Even surgeries can end up feeling this way. And at the end of the day, after all this, you leave the clinic, arrive home exhausted, and don't even realize you've just spent three hours watching Netflix.

It feels like groundhog day. Like you're just going through the motions but nothing changes—and in reality, nothing actually does. *If you are living in your subconscious, you are just re-creating more of what you have already experienced.*

Thankfully, you can break this cycle by reprogramming your subconscious mind! As suggested to me by my mentors, reprogramming your thoughts during adulthood can happen in two ways:

- Extreme emotional events

- Repetition

Extreme emotional events instantly rewire your subconscious thinking because they immediately form a new paradigm. Unfortunately, they aren't particularly useful as an intentional rewiring tool because these events are unpredictable and oftentimes traumatic. Think of touching a hot stove as a young child as one of your earliest extreme emotional events.

A few years ago, I experienced my own version of an extreme emotional event that altered the course of my life forever.

Enter Diablo!

I'll admit, given everything we see and deal with as veterinarians, this occurrence was fairly innocuous. I have dealt with every demeanor of animal and have been hit with every form of animal discharge at one point or another—this just happened to have arrived at the right time and in the right way.

Over the course of years, my thinking patterns had become negative most of the time, and Miserable Mike was born. Once I became aware of this, the task of unwinding it all seemed insurmountable because I had no clue how to break free of him. I'd have brief flurries of motivation, but no lasting results.

The negative momentum continued on and on like a feedback loop until I finally reached full-on desperation. It was from this emotional state that I experienced this event.

To be honest, I forgot the real cat's name, so let's just say Diablo's moniker was...demeanor based. This cat was 20lbs of pure, absolute fury. At any second, he could explode and utilize his multiple weapons to inflict as much damage as possible on any poor unsuspecting soul.

In the waiting room, Diablo seemed to be a perfectly friendly and well-behaved tomcat, but we quickly discovered it was all a ruse. Diablo sprang into action in the treatment room, and, in a blink, had successfully drawn blood from one of the technicians that was holding him. His deadly assault continued. I can't quite place exactly what I saw as limbs flailed about and Diablo yowled out his war cry, but I did *feel something*. And tasted it too...

Diablo had managed to empty his entire bladder on my face.

As cat piss ran down my face and across my tastebuds, I vividly remember standing there in the treatment room, frozen, and completely knowing: *I am done. That's it.* I just knew.

It was as if in that moment all of the excuses and limiting beliefs I had been telling myself took a back seat. I knew the direction of my life had immediately shifted forever. Thinking back to the scalpel blade analogy, I made a decision. It was time for me to cut into investing so that I could have control over my life and inspire others to do the same. The necrotic tissue that I needed to debride was clinical practice itself.

A few days later I debriefed this event with my personal coach over our regular Zoom call. I retold the story of Diablo with my gaze hanging low. When I finally looked up at the computer screen my coach had three dates written down, all in the near future.

"Pick one," he said. And so, I did.

That was the date I was to hand in my resignation letter. I had it typed up later that evening and so it was that July 17, 2018 was to be my last clinical shift as a veterinarian. Immediately after finishing that letter, before it was even handed in, ideas and visions about my future came pouring in. Among those ideas was *The Veterinary Project* podcast and this very book.

I've heard similar stories from other veterinarians. The actual event that finally triggers that definitive decision varies, but the common denominator is that they are suddenly confronted with the difficult internal work they have been avoiding because there simply is no other option.

Although extreme emotional events can cause a certain desperation that makes change necessary, they happen spontaneously as I've noted above—which is not something you can rely on (e.g. car accidents, health diagnoses). This brings me to the more predictable second suggestion: repetition, or habits.

Because habits are basically our thoughts and feelings in action, they are the key to adjusting behaviors and identity. In other words, if you can change your habits, you will change your life. I have spent years identifying habits that no longer serve me so I can replace them with ones that do.

Habits are an essential tool in reprogramming your subconscious.

When it comes to habit reformation, you need to shift your identity to *be* the person you want to be, then commit to doing what that person would do. For an in-depth dive into this subject, I recommend you study James Clear's *Atomic Habits*[27].

A Plan for Change

My hope is that you now have a few ideas and techniques that can help you embrace change. The next step, realizing the actual change, is the hardest part. Essentially, these skills are nothing without a method to incorporate them.

This brings me to the "Teachability Index," a theory put forward by Kevin Trudeau in his audio series *Your Wish is Your Command.*

Teachability Index = Willingness to Learn + Willingness to Accept Change[28]

You will have to learn how to work with this formula if you ever want to change, but first, I'll explain how it works with an example.

Think back on your journey to becoming a veterinarian. During this period of your life, your teachability index was through the roof because you had a high willingness to learn.

Your schedule was full all day, every day, with lectures and labs. You sacrificed time with friends and family to prioritize your studies. You probably also had a high willingness to accept change as you instantly surrounded yourself with a new cohort and may have moved to a new city.

This proves that you are more than capable of having a high teachability index. You've done it before!

The catch is that we all have a different teachability index in various areas of our life. That's why there are brilliant veterinarians who are also fools with their money, have left a series of failed relationships in their wake, and/or neglect their health.

We have the knowledge and ability to excel *in any area* of life we wish to, but what's much harder is finding the belief in ourselves to do so.

Therefore, the first step in increasing your teachability index in a certain area of your life is to *increase your desire.* But how can you do that?

Think back again to the time you spent becoming a veterinarian. What was one of the first things you did? You spent time with *veterinarians!*

Thus, being in proximity to those that are doing what you want to do is the first step in raising your desire and consequently raising your teachability index. Proximity increases our belief that we can do it too because we get to see with our very own eyes that it is possible! This is why, when we align ourselves with like-minded people, mentorship and masterminds are so powerful. More broadly speaking, both socially and professionally, it's also why diversity and inclusion beget more diversity and inclusion, which can only be a positive thing.

Next, in order to continue, we must break down the teachability index into its two parts—*willingness to learn* and *willingness to accept change.* Let's start with willingness to learn, which can be broken down further into two questions:

What are you willing to do?

What are you willing to give up?

To uncover the identity that already exists within you, you must create space for it by getting rid of the past habits. Too often, we desire the new but aren't willing to let go of the old.

These are the devilishly minute details that can affect your teachability index.

Whenever I consult veterinarians who want to change, I often ask, "Are you willing to give up worrying about what others may say? Are you willing to give up what *you* think others think about you? Are you willing to give up any potential guilt? Are you willing to possibly give up that nice comfortable paycheque that arrives every two weeks? Are you willing to give up certain people in your life? And are you willing to let go of things that are good because you are going for great? Because all of these may be necessary."

These are emotionally difficult questions to face, and you don't need to answer them to anyone but yourself. But you must answer honestly if you want your desire for change to grow.

With this first part of the teachability index in check, let's now focus on the second part, *willingness to accept change*. You will often get a resounding, "Yes!" when you ask people if they want things to change in their life. But that very same group will collectively agree that they don't actually want to commit to making the changes.

Clearly there's a paradox here.

As I touched on earlier, extreme emotional events are one way that space opens up because they are rooted in *desperation*. Desperation is what emotionally charged me into action. Desperation can be a catalyst to change.

But *inspiration* is what keeps you going.

Think of inspiration as something entirely separate from motivation; motivation is fleeting—it fades when life tests you in unpredictable ways—but inspiration does not. Inspiration lasts because it is founded in your identity and core values—in the person you commit to being.

Therefore, as you work on expanding your willingness to accept change, focus on inspiration. Inspiration is enduring.

A Word of Caution

Entire industries have been created around the premise of selling people the idea that they can do the work for you! They promise that, if you take their course, you will finally be able to do everything you could ever dream of.

However, true transformational change must come from

within.

Certainly, there are coaches and mentors and courses that can help guide you, but ultimately, they need to meet certain requirements.

- You must have a high teachability index to change

- You must be able to trust them

- You need to know that they have your best interests in mind

- They must have previously done the thing they are teaching

I have and will continue to surround myself with mentors and coaches (and take the occasional course) with the caveat that the teacher has achieved the results I desire.

You'd never come to see me to learn about horse lameness, for example (I'm definitely in the bottom 1% of veterinarians in this category), instead you would seek out someone who continually worked to master their craft. This applies to veterinary medicine, health, nutrition, finance, investing, or for any area in which you might seek a mentor.

Just remember that no one can grant you the "key" to changing your life, because it doesn't exist somewhere out in the world. It's within you.

Things Don't Happen to You, They Happen for You

I had just stolen the hockey ball and was charging forward on a breakaway. I made a deke to the left and then came back across to my right on my backhand.

This was a move that I'd had success with over the years, but something felt different this time. After pushing off my left leg, I suddenly collapsed to the floor. I wasn't exactly sure what had happened, but I instinctively clutched my leg at the knee. I was writhing around in pain, rolling side to side, and trying to hold back my tears. In that moment, I didn't know what was damaged, but I knew it was bad.

Ball hockey has been my main sport for the better part of a decade. Most of the year it's just recreational, but in the summer I'm part of our provincial team that plays at the national level.

Lying there, writhing in pain, it quickly dawned on me that there was no way I was going to play at the nationals that year. And it turned out I was right.

I would require surgery, many weeks off work, and approximately a two-year recovery to get back to my new version of normal.

I was pissed. The last thing I wanted was to be stuck on a couch for months at a time away from sports and my real estate ventures.

But, I thought, *if I could go back and change my decision, I'd still go in on that breakaway every single time.*

This happened in 2017—a true turning point for me. I was continually moving at lightspeed—trying to balance my veterinary career, my and my wife's growing real estate portfolio, and all of life's other demands. I never took time off because I didn't see it as an option.

But when the twisting and snapping of a handful of ligaments happened, I miraculously had all the time I could ever hope for. Something about that terrified me. What was I going to do with all this time?

I surprised myself in the resulting weeks of recovery following my surgery. They were some of the most productive in my life—not in a traditional "work" way, but in an introspective way. I was also able to attend conferences on real estate, study up, and network within the industry. I reflected on myself, my life, and my goals and realized I was done not living for myself. Done with having regrets. Done with resenting the person I'd become. I used my new-found time to read, research, and clarify what I desired.

In retrospect, I understand now that I hadn't been creating space for myself in my life—so the universe did it for me.

Most importantly of all, I made a decision: Miserable Mike would disappear, and he would *never* come back. With that, I'll leave you with some pieces of advice I gained throughout the process of leaving him behind. Here we go.

It's Your Responsibility to Make the Decision to Change

In every situation, no matter how disappointing things are in the moment, there are opportunities. Doors may close, but others open that can lead you to something greater.

During my career as a clinical veterinarian, I often felt as though I was swimming against a raging river—no matter how hard I tried, I couldn't change it.

There were endless appointments to see, responsibilities that weren't part of my job, and communications fires to put out. It was so easy to never change because I was caught up in everything else. In fact, with the benefit of hindsight, I now know that I kept myself preoccupied so that I would never have to face the internal work required to change.

Look in the Mirror

"It's not my fault." How many times have you thought that?

When I was a practicing vet, I would think to myself, "Why would the receptionist book that appointment at that time?" or, "I can't believe that client said that! There is no way I'm doing that!" I was constantly a victim.

But one thing that changed my perspective and has literally

changed my life is the idea we first talked about in Chapter 6: you are 100% responsible for everything in your life. Truly embodying this belief *no matter the situation.* Yes, there will be times and events when clearly outside factors are at play. But your life takes on a whole new level when you put that aside and own it all.

As I recovered from my knee surgery, I had to face the cold hard truth. Everything that I had done in my life—all of the thoughts and decisions, the actions, and the inaction—had resulted in me being exactly where I was. If I was looking for anyone to blame, it was me.

And finally:

Take Action Toward Your Vision

As Philip McKernan, a mentor of mine, says, "In the absence of clarity, take action." Even when you're not certain of your ultimate destination, taking action is better than being stuck in a place you don't want to be.

Personally speaking, I had to take massive action to jar my life in a different direction. While recovering from my injury, I dove in and studied everything about myself: personal development, finances, and so on. I put every aspect of my life under the microscope. I made a strong commitment and took a massive amount of action.

I don't want to make it sound unduly difficult, but in many ways this was some of the hardest work I have ever done. I began with networking and joined a mastermind group, surrounding myself with like-minded people. Since early 2019 and still to this day, every Monday night I have a Zoom meeting with six other people across the world. We support, encourage, and challenge each other. This group has, and continues to be, life-changing for me.

I also continued to find ways I could move myself and my life into greater alignment. One of those ways was diving fully into real estate investing and stepping away from clinical veterinarian medicine practice. Don't worry—you don't have to do that! Just find what works for you.

Shifting your identity so it aligns with you and who you desire to be is critical. In her book, *The Top Five Regrets of the Dying*, Bronnie Ware lists the number one regret as, "I wish I'd had the courage to live a life true to myself, not the life others expected of me."[29]

I truly hope that everyone reading this book never knows that regret.

Chapter Nine

Curate Your Environment

I N OUR PROFESSION, there is no end to the requests, demands, or areas where our time and energy is needed. If you need proof of this, just look at how far out you and/or your veterinarian friends are booked! Just booking three busy veterinarians for an episode of *The Veterinary Project* podcast feels like trying to herd feral cats.

Just like you should put on your own oxygen mask first before helping others on a flight, veterinarians must put themselves first to ultimately support their patients. If you look at it that way, tending to your needs first isn't selfish—doing so will actually allow you to help the greatest number of people and their pets.

At the same time, I believe that we as veterinary professionals already know this. We've read all the memes about how you can't pour from an empty cup and heard the oxygen mask in an airplane analogy before. Why, then, is self-care so challenging?

It all comes down to environment. If you can get both your internal and external environments aligned, your self-care will come naturally.

Internal and External Environment

Firstly, I believe the way we've learned to think about self-care is all wrong. Every article you read seems to say the same thing. They'll talk about how important it is, list some habits you should employ daily, and wish you good luck on your way out of the browser. Thankfully, that's not the approach we're going to be taking right now.

Instead, we'll focus on how your environment can impact your growth and, therefore, self-care. In Chapters 7 and 8 we looked at identity and concluded that if we're not seeing results (such as when we *say* we want to practice more self-care, but don't), it is often because we don't have our thoughts and feelings/emotions in alignment with our identity. Once you have your identity in alignment—which is what I call your *internal environment*—you need to then focus on your *external environment*—more on this later. We are constantly creating our external environment while, at the same time, it is constantly providing feedback and shaping us too. Consequently, if your external environment doesn't match who you commit to being, you have to do something about it.

Being able to successfully align your environments is the result of doing two things: first, aligning with your internal environment, and then removing any resistance you may be experiencing in your external environment. I know this idea may come across as complicated, but it'll make sense soon—I promise.

Habits

Habits can be an incredibly useful tool when you want to align your identity/internal environment with your external environment. The trick is picking the right habits. What usually happens is that people pick habits that aren't right for them, so they become destined to fail. Maybe they'll fake it for a while or temporarily change their behaviors, but it never lasts. However, when the habit is something they truly desire, their actions will align with their identity.

In other words, identity must propel action.

If you want to be vegan, you must eat vegan food. If you want to be a swimmer, you must swim. Whatever it is you want to be, you must *do the work to become it*—and habits can get you there.

You can't just go through the motions that you hope will make you the person you want to be. Instead, you must embrace the bigger shift that happens once you believe you are already that person (meaning your thoughts and feelings are in alignment) and then just do what that person does. The habit no longer becomes a "to-do" on your list, it's altogether a new way of "being."

For example, I wanted to embrace running and build a habit out of it. I did what most people do and made it a habit to run every day, even though it was tough, and I didn't consider myself a runner. Don't get me wrong, this was a good start to a new habit in my life, but if I had continued running this way, I would have given up.

To continue forward, I realized I would have to stop "running" (for the sake of running) and become "a runner." Running would have to become a part of my identity, otherwise I would lose interest in it.

I had to do some of the internal work we talked about in the last two chapters (e.g. deciding *I am a runner*). I became more self-assured, my running identity was uncovered, *and then* I became a runner[30].

Runners run, and equally, coffee drinkers drink coffee. They don't need to think, *Gee, I want a coffee right now*, wait until they feel like they want one, and then drag themselves up to go make one. They just do it automatically because that's who they are!

In short, habits are kind of like the bridge between a person's internal environment (A.K.A. their identity) and their external environment (which we will focus on next). Habits reside in both spheres—therefore the goal of a habit must be tied to your identity in some way if it's going to last (unless you want it to be short-term).

The next time you pick a habit to work on, take care to be discerning and choose one that's aligned with who you want and commit to being. You'll know what that is because it's the difference between the task being a "to-do" versus it "being yourself."

Externally Aligned

Something magical happens when you go one step further with identity and habits by making your external environment align with your internal one. For me, this looked like moving to a location near a river so I could run beside it, and changing our basement—which used to have a pool table and bar—into a yoga space and gym.

The following tips will help you do either one or both of these things: get your external environment further aligned with your internal one, or remove any resistance to alignment you may be experiencing. In other words, they will help you continue to "be," not just "do." Start by:

- Looking at your social circles

- Finding an accountability partner

- Letting "No" make way for "Yes"

- Ruthlessly assessing

One of the greatest external environmental shifts I made was to adjust who I was surrounding myself with. The mastermind group I told you about last chapter eventually became a social circle that deeply affected me for the good.

Every time we met, I listened to their thought processes, got updates on what they were up to, and saw them get results. Suddenly, I knew anything was possible. Even better, they helped increase my confidence because they supported me, encouraged me, and believed in me when it came to my endeavors.

It's a similar idea to when Roger Bannister became the first person to run the four-minute mile, shattering the world's belief that a sub four-minute mile was humanly impossible. As soon as he broke that barrier and proved to everyone that it was possible, other athletes immediately started to break it as well.[31] They now believed it was possible and so they did it.

When you're armed with first-hand accounts from incredible people like I was, your personal desire begins to increase, which translates to an increase in your willingness to learn and willingness to accept change as well (i.e. the teachability index). For example, you want to be around a veterinarian team that takes care of themselves and encourages your well-being, too—which means, for example, that you will take that lunch break. Similarly, I bought my first apartment building because I was around people who had done it before; I also left the traditional nine-to-five because I put myself around others who had also done that.

Once you are willing to learn and accept change, you are finally able to let go of old thought patterns and step into new ones. The best part about stepping into these new thought patterns is that new actions (and results) follow.

For all these reasons, I highly recommend that you **asses your social circle** (this includes family, organizations, and work) and determine if they represent who you commit to being. If not, change it. This may require you to cut some people off, but most of the time it will just involve you adjusting the dial on who you spend time with.

On a similar note, the second piece of advice I have is to **find an accountability partner**.

It's no surprise that the more you push outside of your comfort zone, the more you'll want to revert to that comfort zone. As humans, it's just in our nature to avoid fear, danger, and the unknown. Not doing so could lead to irreversible consequences in the wild, after all!

Fortunately, we don't need to think that way anymore.

That's why it can be extremely helpful to find a "buddy" for support as you start a new journey. Maybe this is a friend who you trust and is on a journey of their own—like trying to eat clean or detox themselves of some bad habit. Whatever it is, you can be their rock during their transformation, as they can be yours. You can use their continual push until your comfortable mean resets at a new level.

Another option for accountability can be through a personal coach or mentor, both of which have served me well over the years. The caveat here is that whoever you work with must be aligned with your personal core values—morally and ethically. Otherwise, you'll just be wasting time and money. It will feel like you're working really hard, but in reality you won't be getting any closer to your goal because you and your coach won't have that deep understanding that comes with being aligned.

Next, when it comes to adjusting your external environment, you must **learn to say "No" from time to time**. I think this just might be the hardest thing for us veterinarians to do because we are so used to saying "Yes."

But the thing is: "*No" makes way for "Yes.*"

Bob Proctor's "Vacuum Law of Prosperity" states that no two

things can occupy the same space at the same time. In practice, what this means is that if we remove something from our environment a vacuum of space will be created that will be filled by something else. Saying "No" to one thing allows us the space to say "Yes" to something else.[32]

When this is applied to our external environment, most of us have this concept backwards. We will only say "No" after we have procured the sufficient "Yes" replacement. I received my PhD in the Vacuum Law of Prosperity in the most memorable—and embarrassing—way.

LET the bed bugs bite

For as long as I can remember I wanted a king-sized bed. Anytime Rosalie and I would stay at a hotel we'd book a room with a king-sized bed and marvel at all the space we had and how incredibly we slept. We'd return home to our queen-sized bed and lament how we had no room. This was further accentuated by Riley's arrival and her frequent overnight visits into our bed. I'd wake up with Riley's foot in my face and have nowhere to escape to as I couldn't possibly slide over any further. Without realizing it, I was violating the Vacuum Law of Prosperity.

You see, no king-sized bed would ever enter our bedroom while we still had this perfectly good queen-sized bed. Sure, we wanted to upgrade but we had no urgency. We already had an expensive high-quality mattress and we *needed* somewhere to sleep. Once we found the king-sized bed we wanted, we would throw this one out. A very logical line of reasoning, but ultimately wrong.

Then, some tiny intruders, likely stowaways from one of my many real estate trips, kicked the Vacuum Law into motion and I witnessed first-hand how powerful it can be.

"Yes, these are bed bugs!" exclaimed the exterminator as he ran his magnifying glass along the bottom seam of our bed. Rosalie and I stood at the doorway in horror. We had been tipped off by some red bite marks on my legs and some strange insect we couldn't quite place a few days before. Within minutes, and I mean at lightning speed, our entire master bedroom was empty. The bed we refused to let go was out on the front lawn ready for its ultimate delivery to the landfill.

And in the following weeks something magical happened. Our bedroom was replenished with all the pieces we had always wanted—including our king-sized bed!

With a better grasp of the Vacuum Law of Prosperity, I now immediately remove items in my external environment that cause resistance or do not serve me. You can't just hope to start being your new self—you must actively create space for it and trust that that space will fill in alignment.

Furthermore, only when you start saying "No" and stop living in a reactionary environment where you say "Yes" to everything that is thrown at you can you live a life that you design—that you *believe* you deserve, and one that reinforces your internal identity.

Saying "No" prevents us from wasting time and energy on activities that don't serve us, so that we can dedicate more time to activities that *do* serve us and enjoy the impact we are creating. In this way, positive momentum builds, and so does a positive sense of self-worth.

Saying "No" to an environment that does not serve you also leaves you with the space and freedom to finally say "Yes" to the right environment. You'll know which is which because the right external environment, once aligned with your internal identity, will propel you forward, whereas the wrong one will drag you down.

Lastly, once we understand that our environment either propels us or restricts us, and at the same time has the power to influence our identity, we start to take things around us a lot more seriously. This means you'll have to **ruthlessly assess**.

Our external environment can be broken down into countless micro-environments, where each either serves you or doesn't. Your home environment includes places where you sleep, work, play, relax, cook, eat, socialize, and so on—so set yourself up for success in each of them!

One of my biggest pet peeves of all time is a T.V. in the bedroom! Your bedroom is for sleeping (and for one other thing, *wink*), so a T.V. only creates resistance to our goal of having a great night's sleep. In the same way you approach definitive decision-making, make bold, conclusive decisions around your environment, and only make them once. If you don't ever put a T.V. in your room, you don't have to make the nightly decision to not watch it.

Similarly, our veterinary environment can fall under the same magnifying glass. We are now seeing environments shift to support our ultimate visions—for example, moving phones away from the front entrance so a client isn't greeted by someone trying to juggle a phone call, collect payment from the previous customer, and check in the next patient. The customer's first and last impression can be much more pleasant and the front receptionist much more efficient.

In summary, ruthlessly assess your external environment so it aligns with your internal one. For instance, if you love surfing—and want *to be* a surfer—move close to the beach. It sounds simple because it is!

You Intuitively Know

You may have noticed that this chapter was fairly light on specific self-care actions. That is because no one knows you like *you*! You intuitively know what you need. You simply have to learn to honor that. The specific action can be whatever speaks to you. But ultimately, for that to happen, the key is to get your internal and external environments aligned and optimized, and remove any areas of resistance.

Chapter Ten

You Can Do Hard Things

IF THERE IS one area of veterinary medicine that I got blatantly wrong in my early years, it was resiliency. Immaturity, mixed in with a healthy dose of twenty-something male ego, led me to the amazingly wrong conclusion that resiliency was simply about capacity. The ability to carry the case load, no matter the overwhelming volume, without showing even the slightest sign of cracking.

Boy, was I wrong!

My understanding of resiliency was limited to the attitude of, *Bring on all the cases...resiliency is either something you have or don't have, and I have it!* Unfortunately, I think most vets can relate to the idea of feeling like they must be able to, or at least appear to be able to, handle everything that comes their way. Internally, we may still be incredibly overwhelmed, but feel compelled to not let any of it show to the outside world. There is an underlying fear that comes along with this thinking: the belief that, deep down, if you aren't able to push through and do *all* the work, you are not worthy as a vet.

It wasn't until I started studying researcher and educator Dr.

Robyne Hanley-Dafoe's material that a true picture of healthy, lasting resiliency formed in my mind.

According to Dr. Hanley-Dafoe, there are *five core competencies* that make up your baseline resiliency.[33] I used to believe resiliency was something you either had or didn't, but the good news is that these core competencies are learnable and can be developed, even if you are starting from as misguided a place as I was.

My previous understanding of resiliency was extremely rigid—it was about acting like you can handle everything without wavering or getting knocked down. With this thinking, if you bend, you will break.

In contrast, Dr. Hanley-Dafoe's model is much more gentle, denoting that there are ebbs and flows in resiliency—periods where you do get knocked down, but get back up again when you are ready. You can bend, and that's OK.

Her five core competencies of resiliency are:

1. Belonging

2. Perspective

3. Acceptance

4. Hope

5. Humor[34]

In studying these competencies and analyzing my own veterinary experiences, I gained clarity around veterinary resiliency. I didn't know what resiliency was before, but because of Dr. Hanley-Dafoe's model, I learned that it is OK—indeed it's necessary—to take pitstops in order to achieve a more sustainable career.

Belonging

"What?! You've got to be kidding me!" Those were the only words my buddy could get out amidst his thunderous laughter.

We were out having some beers for our quarterly meet up; this one just happened to be over the Christmas holidays. Given that we were vet school classmates, we liked to get together and shoot the breeze about how things were going.

Everyone in the bar probably thought I had just told him a hilarious joke or story, but this was not the case. He was the only one laughing, while I sat there, staring into my beer.

I had just told him about the Christmas bonus and gift I had received from my employer: a pair of those thin, stretchy dollar store mini mitts and a $50 gift card. To say I was disappointed was an understatement.

When his laughter finally subsided, he gave me his perspective as a vet clinic owner. "I know I was laughing, but I'm sorry—I've always thought Christmas time was the perfect opportunity for an owner to show their staff just how valued and important they are. That's what I try to do every year."

He then shared with me what he had given his staff. Needless to say, it far exceeded what I had received and left me feeling even angrier than before.

Because I didn't want that anger to grow any further, I didn't tell my buddy that I had also sacrificed two of my four days off over Christmas to go into the clinic and perform a few urgent surgeries. Even worse, my lack of boundaries caused tension at home because it delayed our plans to go visit family. And all of this occurred without so much as a thank you from clinic ownership and management.

That's what *really* had me fired up.

It had nothing to do with the Christmas bonus. In all honesty, the Christmas bonus could have been any amount and it still wouldn't have changed how I felt in that situation. It did, however, make me realize one thing: something wasn't right.

Having a sense of belonging for where you work is incredibly important. It follows, then, that perhaps the reason I had missed the mark so amazingly for understanding resiliency was because I completely ignored this first pillar.

During the majority of my career, I was ignorant to my sense of belonging in a clinic setting. I had mislabeled this as feeling unappreciated, but never bothered to dig any deeper into why I felt that way.

Instead, I took the easy escape and blamed it all on money—a complaint I was happy to make to anyone who would listen. I eventually grew resentful of the case load and working long and seemingly hard hours.

But I didn't feel this way at every clinic I worked at. I spent several years doing locum work at a clinic that was aligned with my core values, where I felt real appreciation and a sense of true belonging. Interestingly, at this clinic an even more intense case load landed differently with me. I felt cared for, appreciated, and understood. There was never any resentment because we were all in it together. Oftentimes, I would leave after a long day and actually feel rejuvenated.

That was *belonging* at work.

Further proof of the power of belonging can be heard in other vets' accounts. Multiple guests on *The Veterinary Project* podcast highlight having a sense of belonging at work as a significant contributor to their success and well-being. Conversely, the most common complaint I hear (and one I have certainly been guilty of issuing) is, "I work in a toxic vet clinic." Belonging and toxicity seem to be at opposite ends of the veterinary clinic environment spectrum.

Something that helped me change my mindset about the "toxicity" of my environment was the realization that each individual is responsible for their relationship to their environment. We *can* influence it.

This brings me to the idea of *creating your own belonging*.

A toxic team has toxic individuals in it. This means it is our individual responsibility to look in the mirror and honestly answer if we are showing up as the best version of ourselves or as one of these toxic individuals. Are we creating an environment of belonging? Or allowing a toxic environment to influence us?

As an individual, you have to realize that a problematic culture isn't going to improve if you have poor leadership and don't do anything about it.

Create your own belonging.

Actively influence all environments that you are in toward the positive. Speak up for yourself and others—or leave. Whatever you do, don't just do nothing.

At the same time, individuals can only do so much, and, ultimately, belonging must first exist collectively before it will be experienced individually. In other words, until a sense of belonging permeates an entire vet clinic, it can't be magically felt by an individual.

The truth is that veterinary clinics that operate as a close team or family that shares the same core values, mission, and purpose will rise above the rest. There are many amazing veterinary leaders out there that are actively creating these environments. You deserve to feel as though you belong, not as though you are just trying to fit in.

Perspective

Dr. Hanley-Dafoe talks about perspective in terms of full body awareness. It's not just about intellectually viewing something with our eyes and interpreting it with our brain, but also about listening to our gut feelings and intuition.

The entire notion of "perspective" has morphed tremendously for me over the years.

I used to think that perspective was entirely made up of mindset, and while this is partially true, a different kind of understanding can be reached when we look beyond just the mind. In reality, a lot of perspective is about listening to your intuition—or, in other words, getting your mindset (which is in the head) and *soulset* (which is in the gut and heart) aligned, as coined by Philip McKernan.

Therefore, when you want to shift or expand your perspective, you first need to focus on connecting with both your mindset *and* soulset.

Most people find mindset easier to understand because it's the "logical" part of us, but tend to struggle with soulset. I think this is because our mindset (or thoughts) often speaks to us via language, where as our soulset (gut and heart) is more feeling-based. Connecting the two can be powerful. In the veterinary clinic, this could be something as simple as that quick pause to notice our hunger pangs, or more complex, and something I have personally experienced, such as a deep yearning for simplicity.

The point here is that there is more than just our brain helping us filter our world.

To work on your soulset, you need to first give yourself space. Dedicate time to just be and to quiet your thoughts. To learn to actually feel your feelings. For me, getting out into nature completely unplugged is the most favorable environment.

The next, and biggest, step to improving soulset is to honor these epiphanies. A major one that I experienced was my decision to *not* buy a veterinary clinic back in 2012. My mind could endorse the investment with all sorts of positive justifications, but ultimately, I knew in my gut that it wasn't the right move for me at that time. Real estate investing felt much more aligned. This step cannot be overstated because sometimes it defies logic. I have conversations with veterinarians who are regularly faced with this exact same dilemma. A veterinarian purchasing a veterinary clinic *makes sense* logically, but that still doesn't mean it makes sense intuitively.

Resiliency comes into play here as we learn to honor our mindset and soulset.

For example, my old thoughts about resiliency would've told me to skip lunch so I could work more. I thought it was weak to do otherwise. This was driven exclusively by mindset. Because I have an expanded perspective today, I would say that it's more resilient to take your breaks and eat your lunch so that you can think more clearly and sustain yourself for your working day and, ultimately, for a fulfilling career.

My overall perspective was poor for a good portion of my veterinary career. I would only focus on the negative events of the day, feel sorry for myself, and then find myself unable to let those negative events go. Playing the victim card can lead to a very negative downward spiral.

A dramatic shift occurred when I began my daily gratitude, which includes writing in my "gratitude journal." This simple, conscious intention to shift my focus away from the negative and over to the positive—the same positive that had always been there but that I had ignored—significantly changed my perspective for the better.

From there I took my perspective one level deeper, starting with an awareness of my intuition, then slowly beginning to trust my gut and intuition. This is still a work in progress, but so far it has served me well to honor what I feel is intuitively right for me. I have become more resilient by stepping out of my comfort zone when my gut calls for it.

As Dr. Hanley-Dafoe says, "If life didn't challenge us, it wouldn't change us. It is important to trust the process of growth and accept that we are well equipped to move through challenges and change."[35]

Acceptance

I think all vets know deep down that they're eventually going to face a case that ends in the unexpected death of the patient. Knowing this is one thing—the hardest part is accepting it.

I am no exception. When I first experienced the unplanned passing of a patient in my early career, I found myself emotionally frozen. It was one of those things you just can't learn how to handle from a textbook.

As terrible as something like this is, you will never be able to grow from it until you actually experience it. You must learn acceptance. It is immensely freeing once you let go and accept that you will make mistakes and that there will always and often be things outside of your control. This reality is also true: some animals will die no matter what we do.

Dr. Hanley-Dafoe frames acceptance as acknowledging what has already happened and shifting our questions from focusing on the past (why) to action-oriented and future-focused questions (how and what). Ultimately, I found the general concept of accepting that which you have no control over easy to grasp intellectually but challenging to put into practice. I have certainly been guilty of ruminating on past events for far too long.

Here are some things that have helped me:

1. **Set a limit on how long you get to be emotionally charged.** I realize we may not have exact control over this, but even the act of recognizing my emotions helps me assess the situation. From there I can reasonably give myself the appropriate window of time to vent. It could be five minutes or by the end of the weekend.

2. **During that period, be pissed off, feel sorry for yourself, feel whatever you feel.** Don't judge it; just let the emotions dissipate. I can certainly tell you from years of experience that it is no fun holding them all in.

3. **When your window of time to vent is over, shift to looking forward.** Reframe the event by asking yourself: What can I learn from this? What is great about this? How did this happen *for* me?

Accepting difficult situations leads to growth, perspective shifts, and the willingness to embrace challenges. Over time, as your ability to accept improves, you find you're not knocked down as hard or for as long when something difficult comes your way—this is your resiliency increasing.

One important thing I want to note is that all of the above relates to acceptance *after* something bad happens. In the vet world, this could be learning an animal has passed away overnight. The event is over and nothing can be changed.

But there's another part to acceptance: What happens when you are IN a challenging situation?

An example of this could be getting slammed with multiple emergencies in the clinic all at the same time. As it's happening, it's overwhelming and hard to process, but something that can really help you grasp and understand the situation is *acceptance in the moment.*

Here are some ways I navigate this:

- **Acknowledge that the event is here.** It isn't the time to worry about why it happened or what could have been done differently.

- **Tell yourself that doing hard things is how we grow.** Challenges are not meant to knock you back, they are meant to move you forward—even though it will likely not feel that way in the moment. A few deep breaths will help.

- **Shift to forward thinking and ask yourself how you can move on.** We can almost never see the entire path forward, but we can usually see the next step.

- **Remember: this, too, shall pass.** Your survival rate for everything you have done in your life is 100%. You will get through this and be OK. Once it's over, take some time to acknowledge what you accomplished.

Whatever the outcome—even if you make a mistake—you will grow and learn from the experience.

Hope

When Dr. Hanley-Dafoe was interviewing soldiers returning from service, she found that they often had unfinished home renovation projects. Her research project was focused on seeing if the soldiers were integrating back into society well, so she needed to understand what their weekend plans were.

Most of them had the same response: they were all finishing up a project they had left behind.

After noticing this pattern, Dr. Hanley-Dafoe asked the senior officer about it. His response was, "Doc, I believe those boys leave that as a sign of hope for their loved ones that they are com-ing back."[36]

As humans, we are hardwired to look for threats. It's in our DNA and goes all the way back to caveman days. Clever marketers and news channels know this, which is why negative news sto-ries are so prevalent. Unfortunately, this means we are bombarded with negativity daily.

Ultimately, it takes a real effort and focus on the positive to remain hopeful day after day. But all the effort that goes into being hopeful builds resiliency.

Now, I understand that the idea of being hopeful maybe doesn't come easy in a profession which revolves around identify-ing and diagnosing injury and illness, but that doesn't make it any less important. In the same way we can gain perspective, we can train ourselves to focus on favorable outcomes. We can affect our attitude toward both the cases we see and how we anticipate we will feel throughout the day.

Some of the ways you can do this:

1. Work on your confidence: the ability to be hope-filled—much like decision-making—is enhanced when you are confident. Think about it—if you're confident in yourself, it's only natural that you will view the day ahead and the results of your actions in a more positive light. Confidence makes it easier to choose hope.

2. Cut out negatives. Maybe this means you limit the amount of news, social media, etc. you pay attention to or even cut it out entirely. I've found this helps me in two ways. One, it frees up energy. And two, it makes me less inclined to move to negative thoughts in my own life.

3. Remember that hope begets more hope. This is a pattern

of thinking that we can literally reinforce in our brain through the Reticular Activating System (RAS).

From my own personal growth journey, I think it's amazing that these steps have helped me go from coming in on Mondays with a bad attitude to being hopeful for the day ahead, knowing that it would be full of opportunities to help more people.

Entering each day filled with hope is a recurring choice. And much like many of the topics we've covered, it's your choice to make.

Humor

Sometimes, the joke is on you.

Back in 2010, I was looking for a new job at a few different veterinarian clinics. One clinic invited me to do a one-day job shadow, so I promptly accepted and showed up professional and prepared.

But I was quickly taken aback by the environment. If *stuffy* was a feeling, I was being overwhelmed by it. Over the course of the day, not a single joke or laugh was shared. All doctors addressed each other by their title and last name because first names were not allowed.

It was strictly business. A complete mismatch to my personality.

My philosophy had always been that a good laugh during the day is the easiest way to lighten the load, especially when we work in a profession that can get really heavy at times. Naturally, I did *not* accept their offer.

I still stand by this theory, and it seems that Dr. Hanley-Dafoe would do the same. Her definition of the core competency, humor, is pretty self-explanatory: sometimes we need a simple reminder to step back, take a deep breath, and laugh.[37] Yes, we are doing important work, but finding the humor in everyday life helps to take the edge off and forces us to not to take ourselves too seriously.

The fact that we are doctors and deal with serious medical and surgical cases doesn't mean we can't, or shouldn't, laugh. In fact, I think it's helpful for our often-heavy emotional states to have a laugh if the time and place is appropriate. One surprising benefit of humor is that your resiliency will increase—always being stuck in serious mode is exhausting!

The Time Is Now

One coaching exercise that brought a lot of clarity into my life involved making a simple sketch. Our instructions were to draw a picture of our truth in the future, three years from now.

We were to sketch who we wanted to be. No words were allowed.

The theory behind this exercise was to access new portions of our brain and creativity. We were to give it no thought and simply let the pencil hit the paper and draw. Immediately, I started drawing myself standing on a hill with a huge smile on my face, then I started filling in the spaces on the hill as if they were time stamps on a clock.

I was standing directly on top, at exactly twelve o'clock.

The picture went further to show my thoughts through a thought bubble. Inside it, I drew the exact same picture I had just finished drawing. There I was as a little stick man, smiling from ear to ear, being entirely present in the moment.

I had intuitively known for years that I struggled to be present, but there it was, staring back at me: I craved being present.

This exercise always makes me think of the classic meme explaining why dogs are happier than people. It looks something like this. A person and a dog sit side by side with thought bubbles coming from each of them. The person has multiple thought bubbles going in all directions, displaying all sorts of stress, while the dog has one simple thought: he is only thinking about sitting next to his owner in that exact moment.

Mindfulness

Meditation and mindfulness expert Jon Kabat-Zinn defines mindfulness as, "awareness that arises through paying attention, on purpose, in the present moment, non-judgementally."[38] Take for instance walking into a treatment room to the sound of an IV pump beeping. Mindfulness teaches us to observe the sound, but reserve judgmental thoughts such as, *Who put this catheter in?* or, *Why didn't they place a new bag of fluids?*

Dr. Sara Lazar, a neuroscientist at Harvard, has studied mindfulness and its effect on the brain. Her fascinating research has shown that mindfulness can increase grey matter in multiple areas of our brain such as those responsible for perspective taking, empathy and compassion, and sensory integration.[39] Mindfulness has also been shown to decrease the response in our amygdala, the area of our brain responsible for stress and anxiety.

Dr. Lazar's research suggests that "mindfulness can literally change your brain"![40]

Mindfulness practitioners carry these benefits with them into any environment, including the veterinary clinic. This provides the individual with an enormous opportunity to change their relationship to their environment!

Awareness

After many years of practice, a paradoxical relationship begins to form inside the veterinary clinic: as you become more proficient, you become less aware.

Like anything you have done hundreds or thousands of times,

it becomes repetitive. An increasingly large percentage of your daily tasks start to happen on autopilot, driven by your subconscious mind. When we are operating from this brain space, we are not present and fully engaged.

It goes without saying that if you are intentionally present and mindfully paying attention to your experiences, you will be more aware of how you are feeling. Building on Dr. Hanley-Dafoe's work, mindfulness can help increase your mental strength, but specifically, it can shift your perspective (and soulset). It was this awareness that allowed me to feel and therefore listen to my intuition.

The Past

Lastly, one huge benefit of being present is what it allows us to avoid, which also plays into mental strength, stability, and perspective. When we are present in the moment, we are not in our head reliving a negative past.

I can recall being physically present for countless cat spays while my mind would be wandering around all the endless recesses in my mind. Oftentimes, I would replay conversations with difficult clients or cases that didn't go the way I wanted. Sometimes I agonized over an upcoming decision.

Being present in the moment during these cat spays would have prevented these conversations from playing out endlessly in my mind. The exact same cat spay in the exact same environment, yet my relationship to it could have been entirely different.

Make it a Habit

Further to her five core competencies, Dr. Hanley-Dafoe also outlines a series of micro-habits that help navigate adversity in her paper, "Resilience in Uncertain Times."[41] While they are all valuable, three really jump out at me as being beneficial to a veterinarian.

1. Bookend Your Day[42]

We have discussed the concept of bookending before in this book, but let's go over what it means in this new context.

Really, we can bookend any time period we want to look at. That could mean outlining a three-year vision, scheduling the following week, or working on fostering a miracle morning every day. Veterinary teams could even go one step further and bookend their upcoming daily case load with a quick team huddle. Another idea is to wrap up the day with a brief get together—a chance for the team to reflect on their accomplishments and appreciate themselves.

Regardless of how you bookend, becoming intentional about your day offers an enormous opportunity to foster resiliency in a few different ways. Firstly, bookending helps you set boundaries so you can protect your day, understand upcoming tasks, and foresee potential challenges so you can navigate them easier.

Bookending also gets you to be intentional in advance. Something as simple as creating a verbal intention to yourself before heading into your morning surgeries allows you to set your perspective and be hopeful.

Finally, bookending creates separation from work. It acts as a mental divider, standing in between the working day and home.

2. Protect Your Peace[43]

The external environment of a veterinary clinic will throw challenges at you. There is simply no way to avoid this in such a fast-moving and potentially emotional environment. Eventually you will be triggered, but if you protect your peace you are taking the space you need to ground yourself.

Way back in Chapter 2, I told you about how I would circle around the appointment book and look for appointments that could grant me a moment to breathe while I developed X-rays. That was a technique I used to protect my peace.

Another common technique—that also happens to be a well-known joke—is the fact that many veterinarians will go to the washroom for a few minutes to get some space to themselves (which is a completely valid, but somewhat funny, way to protect your peace). If you're really lucky, you'll be in one of the modern vet clinics that have added a quiet room to the building—thankfully, people are recognizing this need and doing something about it!

No matter what technique you use, know that you can always take a few minutes to yourself, close your eyes, and take a few deep breaths. Peace is within you—you just need to access it.

3. Manage Your Availability[44]

We've all received that awkward social media message from someone we went to high school with, "Hey!! I have this dog…" or the chance grocery store encounter where we're accosted in the produce section and asked to diagnose something based on a few photos. And certainly, we could go in on every single one of our days off and have cases to see.

Resiliency is not seeing how much you can pile on and how far you can go without cracking. Trust me, there is an endless demand for the skills and services you provide as a veterinarian.

If you allow it to, this job will engulf you.

While veterinary medicine is certainly not the only profession that faces burnout, I believe it is vital that we as an industry set better boundaries. We are starting to see dramatic shifts in these areas already, but we must keep looking out for ourselves. No one else is going to.

Your Life Is a Marathon, Not a Sprint

At the end of the day, fostering resiliency is key to those that wish to have long and healthy careers and lives. All the stuff we've talked about so far truly is about practice—not the idea that you either "have it or you don't."

I had this all wrong. I now know that you have to go through setbacks that continue to challenge you so that you can grow and become more resilient. Resiliency is the ultimate tool in your career and life because it simply allows you to get back up. You can take a break. You can pivot. And in the words of Dr. Hanley-Dafoe on *The Veterinary Project*, "You can do hard things."[45]

Resiliency enables us to progressively realize our worthy ideals.

Chapter Eleven

Let's Pivot

So far, you may have noticed that the overarching structure of this book parallels the way a veterinarian's career might look. In the beginning, we focused on all the challenges that begin to layer from "new graduate" to "full-time veterinarian" to "identity confusion" and onwards. Where we are right now is your "midlife crisis"—although it may not be happening in your midlife, and I would argue it isn't a crisis at all.

This is an opportunity.

Pivoting is A Good Thing

I've interviewed around 100 veterinarians so far on *The Veterinary Project* podcast. In 99% of these conversations, our guests talk about how their career has changed over the years. They share with us the path they thought they were going to follow—often what they imagined for themselves when they first decided to be a vet around 16, 18, or 20 years old—and then lay out just how different their journey turned out to be.

Oftentimes, they're still a veterinarian, but just in a different capacity. Kind of like me.

It's important for you to know that not only is it OK for your career to head off on a different trajectory, but that it is also *normal*. When people think of a veterinarian, they tend to imagine only the vet that works in the clinic, but the reality is that this career exists on a spectrum and there's a wide variety of roles you can fill: go into industry, be a business owner or researcher, or, on the more extreme end, become a podcast host.

To be clear, I'm not saying you should constantly pivot every time you feel adversity. As you probably already realize, veterinarian medicine is difficult, so I'm not advocating for you to change direction every time the going gets tough. Instead, I think you know instinctively when you are out of alignment with your career and should choose that time to pivot. If you don't, you may find yourself unhappy, and harboring growing resentment towards your profession. Other times amazing new opportunities simply present themselves with large blinking neon signs begging you to "follow me!" Either way, you will be faced with these forks in the road throughout your career.

How to Pivot

At this point, I hope you see pivoting as something rather inevitable that shouldn't be feared—and that, in most cases, it can be great. The possibilities are endless, and it's exciting to think that you can forge a path in veterinarian medicine that's entirely new.

Here's my advice around pivoting that will help you discover new prospects, change your life, and cope with that change:

- **Put an idea out there and it will manifest.** When you tell others what you want, opportunities will find a way back to you. This was the case for me with real estate—a group of guys I knew were going to look at an apartment, so I asked them if I could tag along. I had no intention of doing anything other than learning and hearing them speak the language of real estate, but then we went out for coffee afterwards, and they told me they needed a third partner on the deal. That turned out to be my first ever apartment building purchase. Oftentimes, amazing things begin with you *just showing up and putting yourself out there*. The perfectionist in you might think you need to have a flawlessly crafted plan, but you don't. Just showing up to begin with can be enough, as it was for me. If you have a passion for a certain area of veterinary medicine, or in any area of your life, start putting it out there! People will notice and you'll find that opportunities will present themselves.

- **Sometimes you must take a few steps backwards to go forwards.** Imagine you're caught inside a maze and that you've just reached a dead end. Are you going to keep walking forward? No! You'll have to go backwards in order to progress. Now apply this logic to being a veterinarian; at the beginning of your career, you had a firm vision for how it would pan out, but the thing is, you're not the same person you were when you first wanted to be a vet in your late teens or early twenties. You will find yourself with new priorities (such as a family, other passions, or simply the desire to not be on-call all the time) that will shift the way you approach your career. But just because a change is happening that makes it *feel* like you're going backwards, it doesn't mean you actually are. This feeling, along with *sunk cost fallacy*—the phenomenon when an individual, group, or organization has a hard time letting something go because they've invested so much time and effort into it—will hold you back if you let it.

- **Productivity does not equal passion.** The chase for extreme productivity and efficiency takes away from the personal connections and relationships you build within your career and could sap the joy from them. Be aware of this trap and leave yourself some space for the magic to happen. I have witnessed appointment blocks shrinking in time and being constantly double-booked becoming more normal. Sometimes a full pivot isn't necessary; it's more about simply rediscovering the joy in your work.

- **Stay curious.** There are endless opportunities in veterinarian medicine, including ones you can create for yourself, so you'll never know what you'll find so long as you remain open to it. On *The Veterinary Project* podcast, we routinely interview guests that are doing something interesting in our industry that we've never heard of before.

- **Love the process.** This is another core tenet of mine that you've heard before. Essentially, I want you to enjoy the rollercoaster that is life, push yourself to appreciate the ups and downs, and reframe thinking that you have failed in some way if you choose to pivot in your career.

While these tips will aid you through the many shapes and forms your career will take, ultimately, some of it will not be within your control. For instance, the opportunity to pivot may simply arrive when it arrives. Sometimes, these profound moments can't come any sooner than they do because you won't be ready for them yet.

Lastly, don't ever be angry at yourself for waiting to change your trajectory. You can't rush the process. In fact, you will have spent the time before pivoting building up your skills and tools— skills and tools that will *allow* you to pivot when the opportunity arises.

In this way, everything is happening *for* you.

Hypoglycemic Change

A client brought her cat into the clinic one day with the hallmark signalment of diabetes. After getting the pet on the exam table, I noticed it had some additional physical exam markers of diabetes including weight loss. With the owner's approval, I ordered all the necessary blood and urine tests.

While waiting for the lab results to come back, I opened a discussion about diabetes with the owner—explaining what it was, what it could mean for her pet, and how we would treat it going forward.

But then the lab results came back.

No signs of diabetes.

Well, what the heck is this, then? My mind raced through all the possibilities while another thought nagged at me. I had told the tech I was working with that I was certain this was diabetes and had *basically just told the owner her cat is diabetic.* Believing I had gone too far down the diabetes road to turn back, I decided to continue with treatment and so prescribed the cat insulin. Two weeks later, the cat had died of hypoglycemia.

Hopefully you picked up on the fact that I am just kidding!

It's hard to imagine that kind of malpractice happening just because a person didn't listen to the signs, respond to new information, or adjust because they believed they had already "gone too far" down one path.

Hopefully my point is coming across crystal clear. Do you see how foolish—and in this case, dangerous—it is to *not* pivot when new information tells you that you should?

I understand that pivoting isn't always easy. While it doesn't just happen, with enough volition and open-mindedness I believe you can craft your life into one that you envision for yourself and absolutely love.

One of the number one constraints I often hear around people making pivots in their life is a lack of financial security. Clearly, it's a valid consideration. Financial independence and passive income gives you more leeway to pivot, which is what we will be focusing on in the next chapters.

Chapter Twelve

The Money Mindset Drain

Before you read this chapter, take a $20 bill out of your purse or wallet and set it in front of you, wherever you are. There's no magic trick involved; I promise.

Just leave it alone until you reach the last page.

ONE DAY IN my 11th grade psychology class, the teacher posed a seemingly random question to the group: "If you were a general in a war, who in this room would you want beside you in a battle?"

Everyone in the class surveyed the room momentarily, until all their eyes fell on two of the biggest and toughest kids in class. The obvious choices, or so I thought.

As this eye game was happening, the teacher meandered up and down the rows of desks. When he saw everyone had settled on their choices, he came to a silent halt next to my desk. He motioned to his choice, and to everyone's surprise—including mine—he was pointing at me.

Me, the scrawny kid with a bad case of voice-cracks and all. It made no sense that he would pick someone that weighed *maybe* 110lbs soaking wet.

Naturally, the class was perplexed and asked for an explanation. The teacher simply stated, "When instructions are given that need to be followed, he listens and executes them."

Sure, it felt good to know that my psychology teacher would trust me to listen and execute a directive, but something didn't sit right with me. *Is that even a good thing? Does that mean I don't think for myself? What am I, a sheep?*

I brushed off the thought and for many years forgot about it entirely. Until one day I realized I had turned into just that, a sheep—but more specifically, a "fiscal sheep."

You see, I was given the "playbook of financial success," and, like most people, I accepted it as the way to thrive monetarily. The rules were really quite simple: get good grades so you can go to university so you can get a good job. *Check, check, and check.*

Like my teacher suggested, I listened to these instructions, and I executed them.

I thought becoming a vet was an excellent way to follow this "playbook of financial success." Although money wasn't really the driving force in my career decision, it was still a factor. I have to admit that I was part of the club that assumed veterinarians were rolling in cash. This translated to me believing that an amazing lifestyle and retirement were a foregone conclusion. There wasn't a doubt in my mind that I was on track to achieve all my financial dreams.

I had no idea just how much financial misinformation was out there.

And so, my question to you is: Who are you going to listen to? Who are you going to let define your financial success?

Reality Strikes

I showed up to work like I did every day early on in my career: with nervous excitement. But something was different that day. Rather, *someone* was different.

If you remember the year 2008, then you know it was a devastating year for financial markets. The good news for me was that I had no money at the time to lose, but many others were not in the same position.

At that point in my life, I saw being the owner of a veterinary clinic as the epitome of success and financial independence. In the short time I had been a vet, I had witnessed a few owners fulfill a distinguished veterinary career, sell their practice, and ride off into the sunset.

But then one day, in 2008, just as the financial markets were tanking and the housing market in the States was collapsing, the previous owner of the clinic where I was working showed up. Not to bring in a pet or to say hello. He was there to work.

He was the owner of the clinic back when I was a student in high school. From what I understood, he had owned it for 30+ years, sold it, and then retired. Now, he was back.

Confused, as I watched him inspect a patient, I wondered, *What's going on?* As I assessed the white lab coat and stethoscope he was sporting, I was taken back to high school, staring at one of the vets I had looked up to as a kid. It all felt a bit unnatural.

It was a surreal moment that stuck with me the entire day. I couldn't shake the bewilderment that bubbled in my stomach every time I walked past him in the treatment room. I felt like I'd seen a ghost.

It wasn't until I took my lunch break, when my workload had dissipated momentarily so I could think, that I pieced it all together. I was largely unaware of just how significant the current financial events were at the time since I wasn't personally invested.

For those that were, it was a bloodbath. And that's when it hit me: *He's not here because he wants to be. He's here because he needs to be.*

When I came to this conclusion, it felt like finding out there's no Santa Claus. Had everything I was taught about personal finance been a lie? I couldn't understand how someone who had followed the playbook perfectly could be back where he started.

He'd had a lifetime career as a vet and was the owner of a flourishing practice. And what was his reward? More work. More financial uncertainty on a road that was supposed to be certain.

Suddenly, I felt the urgent need to project my personal finances forward based on my current salary and compare it to my financial goals. I grabbed a calculator from a nearby desk and started punching out the numbers.

My jaw hit the floor when I saw how many years I would need to work to actually achieve the wealth I desired. It was impossible.

A 150-year target would put me at...well, dead.

Vets Are Behind Before They Even Get Started

After this crushing epiphany, I became obsessed with figuring out how to take charge of my future. This started me on the path to finding financial freedom.

Along the way, I discovered the reasons why vets are struggling at the money game and found new strategies for monetary accomplishment. The biggest shift I underwent was going from thinking you should save up a huge pile of money for retirement and hope to outlive it, to a viewpoint of developing constant streams of income so that you *always* have money coming in and can live how you want, both *today and in the future*. I realized I needed a plan to take me from scarcity to abundance.

In this chapter, we're going to cover the topics that kept me in scarcity:

- Starting from Behind

- Negative Conversations in the Vet Clinic

THE MONEY MINDSET DRAIN

- The Money Mindset Drain

Ultimately, I want you to question the traditional financial view of "exchanging your time for money that you will save in order to someday retire." Instead I want you to think about creating value that generates streams of income that can fund your life both now *and* in the future.

That's why the goal of this "money" chapter is not just to highlight the steps you should take to improve your income. It is also about questioning and potentially changing your *money mindset*—the term I use to encompass all the beliefs one has around money. Only once you have your money mindset in the right place can you begin to see what is available to you.

Furthermore, shifting your money mindset will make all the previous issues we've talked about in this book easier to deal with. You can combat burnout by working less. You can work less when you don't *need* a paycheque. And you don't need a paycheque when you have other sources of income.

I hope what follows will fundamentally challenge the way you think about finances, what is financially possible in your life, and the many paths forward that are available to you.

Starting from Behind

The financial reality of most veterinarians isn't pretty.

Many new graduates enter their career with six figures of student debt. On top of that, they have missed out on years of earning potential due to how long it takes to become a veterinarian in the first place. All of this means that most vets are starting out the money game behind the eight ball.

This contributes to a career full of the issues we've talked about previously. Many vets would love to take more time to rest and recharge, but their finances simply dictate that they need to work more hours. Caught in this vicious cycle, it begins to feel like money controls your life.

And, like most things that have too much control over us, we grow to resent it.

Because we start from behind, it's hard to catch up and pull ahead. This is a significant roadblock to becoming financially free as a veterinarian.

There's a paradox here that further contributes to the problem. Society thinks vets are at a huge financial advantage, but the truth is, we are not.

When we compare our profession to similar ones with lengthy university degrees, like human doctors, dentists, and lawyers, our earning potential is much lower even though it takes a comparable amount of time to earn the degrees. For instance, human doctors can start from behind and still excel financially because their earning potential is exponentially higher.

We could argue about whether or not veterinary professionals are underpaid—believe me I've tried—but the truth is, it doesn't matter. Comparing and complaining doesn't move the financial needle. But it does highlight the fact that we simply need to be more astute than others at personal finance.

For that reason, it is vital that you understand the new money game now!

Negative Conversations in the Vet Clinic

Most people's attitudes and beliefs in all areas of their life are the average of the five people they spend the most time with—and you spend *a lot* of time with your coworkers and clients. By this very reasoning, our thoughts on a particular subject will likely be the average of the opinions we're surrounded by most of the time.

Remember, *we become what we think about, most of the time.*

I have found that conversations surrounding money in the veterinary clinic are, by and large, negative. And because money typically isn't talked about, these exchanges make up 100% of a vet's overall money context.

This kind of exposure to negative thoughts and feelings about money causes vets to focus on and repeat these beliefs until their beliefs start to dictate their actions.

Think about all the discussions you've had regarding money in the clinic. Were they positive or negative? And, most importantly of all, how did these discussions make you feel and affect your attitude toward money?

Personally, it normalized the money struggle for me. Just about everyone seemed to be struggling with their personal finances, so it felt like that was the way it had to be.

But it doesn't.

The Money Mindset Drain

As negative conversations in the clinic continue, reasons to undervalue yourself are reinforced. These thoughts become beliefs; beliefs become actions; and actions become results. Naturally, this chain reaction causes poor financial outcomes, which reinforce negative thinking even further. Certainly, this is far from the financial future we desire. We become stuck and, in extreme situations, our financial situation can continually deteriorate.

The process works like water spiraling down a drain—in other words, *the money mindset drain*.

Generally speaking, the veterinary industry defaults to scarcity when it comes to money. At every clinic I have worked in or visited, the overall tone among the clients and staff whenever money is brought up is considerably more negative than positive. First of all, the subject of money tends to enter conversations when stress and emotions are already elevated. Furthermore, money—or rather, a real or perceived scarcity of it—is often viewed as an obstacle in the way of some desired outcome. And when we come from a place where a resource is limited, it affects our decisions. For example, a scarcity mindset may lead a vet to only offer the least expensive options for a patient's treatment, thereby limiting outcome potentials before they even begin.

I understand why this happens: for vets and clients alike, money is emotion-inducing.

It permeates almost every aspect of modern life and has been directly or indirectly associated with some level of trauma in everyone. It can be a stressor, a blessing, or the bane of someone's existence.

All this baggage makes the conversation around money so difficult. When two people discuss money, they aren't just discussing the physical paper or electronic digits that represent that money, they're bringing an entire *lifetime* of fiscal experiences and emotions to the table.

Money is wrapped in layers of emotion. Think about something bad that has happened to someone's pet—they rush to the vet clinic and unexpectedly get hit with a $1,200 bill they aren't prepared for. The client freaks out because they're confronted with their own money problems, while those communicating with them are reminded of their own anxiety about money.

Furthermore, clients attach a price to your worth and your work. You hear over and over again that veterinary care "costs too much"—that our work isn't worth what we charge for it, or that we force clients to make impossible decisions.

Frustratingly, everyone's emotional biases around money emerge the moment they're forced to discuss it.

It's easy to contribute negative comments about money when

you're surrounded by similar sentiments. But, like everything else in life, you still have to take **100% responsibility** for your own money mindset.

Remember back to when you examined your personal *I am* statements? Well, money conversations work the same way.

When you are repeatedly told something, your subconscious mind grabs it and starts to believe it is true. For this very reason some vet techs, veterinary receptionists, and veterinarians struggle with the belief that they are not worth what they're charging.

After the inner dialogue begins—*Well, that appointment didn't take the full hour, so I'll just charge half the exam fee*—we then bring in all sorts of stories around money and our perceived value. Then we justify charging less, or not even charging at all!

See how a poor money mindset is so limiting?

Money Looms Over You

Starting from behind, negative conversations in the clinic, and the money mindset drain all stand in the way of vets developing an abundant money mindset, but there are also barriers that extend beyond the clinic. Deeper, ingrained reasons that make boosting your finances harder than it needs to be.

If you're ever going to transform your money mindset into one that serves you, you need to identify these reasons and either expel or reframe them. Specifically, I'm talking about everything we consume in our formative years that contributes to our money mindset.

A person's unique money mindset may come from a repetitive narrative that they've accepted over time, or perhaps one intense, emotional event that was related to money. Once these beliefs are firmly embedded in the subconscious mind, it is very hard to abandon them or to not be unknowingly affected by them.

Now is a good time to pause and reflect on your money beliefs to see how they're affecting you and your financial life.

What do you think of when you see the word "money"?

Grab a pen and paper and write down the first five money beliefs that come to mind. You're looking for the first thoughts that cross your mind, so don't spend a lot of time on it. At this point don't worry about *why* you think a certain way—there's no right or wrong! Instead, the aim of this exercise is simply to bring awareness to the beliefs we have around money. Later we can decide whether or not they are serving us.

When you are done, take a look at some of my former money beliefs below (*caution: if you read mine before doing yours, they will bias you!*).

1. **You have to work hard for money.**

This is, unquestionably, the single largest money mindset that I have had to re-wire, and to be honest, I still struggle with this one.

Having grown up on a farm, working hard was a rite of passage and a badge of honor.

In grade school one year, I remember working on an assignment where we had to track every single hour for an entire week to see how much free time we had. The idea being it would highlight that there were no excuses to not do our homework. It just so happened that this assignment was set during harvest time on our farm.

If you come from a farming family, you know that harvest time consists of working as much as you can until the harvest is complete, to the point where a 12-hour day is a short day.

When I'd finished the assignment, my allotment of time labelled "work" absolutely dwarfed every other category. But if I'm honest with myself, I was and still am proud of this character trait. I am not scared to work hard.

But this characteristic comes with one asterisk: I grew up believing hard work meant I had to physically exchange my time for money, with bonus points if the labor was exceptionally difficult. Therefore, anytime I earned money that did not involve me spending a lot of my time or energy, I felt *guilty*.

For example, if I walked into an exam room, could immediately assess that a cat had hyperthyroidism, and came up with a diagnosis and treatment plan in 10 minutes, I would debate with myself about how much to charge. I couldn't accept the idea that I deserved to charge my full exam fee because I got to the diagnosis so quickly, and relatively easily. However, I was discounting the many years of experience and expert knowledge I had—both of which allowed me to recognize the problem and identify solutions in such a short time. I have heard similar stories from many, many veterinarians who feel guilty about charging appropriately, simply because something wasn't difficult or didn't take much time.

Becoming cognizant of the fact that I thought working hard meant I had to spend a lot of time laboring has been the single most impactful revelation of my financial life. I realized that if the only way I earned income was by exchanging my time for money, I would never be free.

Accepting this idea and understanding that I deserve to be paid for the *value* that I provide has changed my life! Value can be created and delivered in many ways, including building systems that literally pay you while you sleep.

2. **People that have lots of money aren't good people.**

It's likely that T.V. and movies are the catalyst for this one.

Just count the many times the antagonist of a story is some rich person who does horrible things to others. Look no further than Ebenezer Scrooge!

I had a fear of becoming a bad person if I became wealthy. For someone who desperately wanted to be liked, being wealthy was not necessarily welcome in my identity. I would wonder, *If I make a lot of money, will others still like me? What will they think of me? What will they say about me?*

I eventually learned to let go of this philosophy. I now believe, from personal experience, that money simply works to magnify character traits that already exist.

If you're a jerk that happens to have money, you will probably be even more of a jerk. If you are a caring and compassionate person, you will probably use your money to do more caring and compassionate things.

3. **I don't deserve to have money.**

I once believed I didn't deserve to have money, or to have any more money than I currently had. This ultimately came from a lower sense of self-worth. For me, linking self-worth and money meant that if I felt a low sense of self-worth, I also felt that I should have a low net worth.

Your net worth is *not* your self-worth, but interestingly, they will probably mirror each other to some degree over a long enough period of time.

Because I tied my self-worth to my paycheque my earnings reiterated my low self-worth. *This is what I've always received, this is how much I'm worth.* I internally programmed myself to put a ceiling on what I deserved.

It became a negative spiral: I never challenged my income, so I never challenged my self-worth. And because I never challenged my self-worth, in turn, I never challenged my income.

This belief was a little harder to identify internally and even harder to expel. I had to really take a hard look at myself, my negative self-talk, and the feelings that weren't serving me. And now that I have let go of this idea, I try to never put an upper limit on myself regarding my self-worth.

4. **It is wrong to want lots of money.**

For most of my life, I felt a sense of shame and guilt because I wanted money.

This belief was mainly rooted in what I thought "money" was or how I defined it. Early on in my career, money was more of a material thing—you can have the nice car or the fancy watch, but it requires money.

What money means to me today is tremendously different. Now I view it as more of a tool that can help me, my family, and others.

Once I acknowledged that I thought it was wrong to want money, I was able to liberate myself from it. I reframed the way I thought about money and started to think of it as a means to do good. Therefore, if I had more money, I could do more good and have more of a positive impact on myself, my family, and the veterinary profession—even the world.

Much like the airline oxygen mask, you need to take care of yourself first before you can take care of others. But once you have that under control, there is truly no limit to how much of an impact you can create.

5. **If I charge for what I do, I am not a good person.**

Ultimately, this belief is a culmination of the first four.

Early in my career as a vet, I often felt the need to discount bills or not charge altogether. I felt like I didn't work hard enough to charge, or I wanted the clients to like me. I felt guilty and didn't value myself enough to charge.

I also found myself falsely reading into external cues that were coming from my clients. I would assume they were upset and start to feel bad, which would justify me not charging them. I would think, *I am taking advantage of them if I do charge them.* I guess I had heard that I was forcing clients to "kill" their pets one time too many, so concluded I was a bad person if I charged for saving their life.

Rebuilding Your Money Mindset

The above list of money mindsets I've overcome is far from exhaustive. However, I hope it has helped to normalize your own list. Going forward, I also encourage you to inspect any moment you get emotional about money, because there may be more money mindset clues buried there. *Curiosity*, not judgment, around our money beliefs is the best tool to help you do this.

If you want to see if your money mindsets are pushing you forward or hindering you, I recommend you try creating a *veterinary vision*, which requires you to imagine what your life could look like in one year, three years, and five years.

For example, my veterinary vision was about controlling my time—not waiting for retirement. I realized that in order to achieve the financial freedom I wanted, I would need to earn money outside of seeing appointments—and I would also need to overcome my five negative money mindsets.

The next step in dismantling and reforming your perspective towards money, now that we have an awareness of our beliefs, is to figure out why we carry these beliefs. Ultimately, the beliefs are just a story we tell ourselves around an event.

Inspecting your history with money is a necessary step in setting a new foundation for positive money mindsets. You need to get all your negative money stories out in the open so you can finally put them to rest and rewrite them.

The Underwear Drawer

Jill's car accident changed my money mindset forever.

The first two weeks following my sister's car accident were centered around the question of if she would survive, so at that stage my parents hadn't given any thought toward what would come next: the road to recovery.

Unfortunately, Jill's recovery presented a lot of financial burdens that my family wasn't expecting or prepared for. One of these costs came from an ongoing legal battle with our insurance company, which refused to pay the automobile accident coverage my family had on Jill.

Another cost was from the two years my mom essentially moved to a different city so she could be with Jill every day while she was in the hospital. The price of food, parking, and travel added up.

Thankfully, Canada covered the medical part of the bill—the cost would've been unimaginable if this hadn't been the case and very likely would've bankrupted our family—but we were still stretched. I was only 10 years old at the time, so the burden wasn't on me financially, but I could still feel it.

My older brother and I fell into a routine where we would visit my mom and Jill on the weekends and stay at home on the farm during the week. We carried on like this for a few months, but one weekend, my mom asked my brother and I to do something that would stick in my memory forever.

When we went home that Sunday, we approached her underwear drawer nervously—we would never otherwise have looked inside my mom's dresser drawers, let alone her underwear drawer. It was clear these were desperate times. I opened the drawer and dug through the garments until there it was, a giant roll of cash that amounted to about $10,000. This was our family's emergency fund.

My brother and I looked at each other and it was clear we were both thinking the same, anxiety-inducing thought: *our family is out of money.*

The feeling of that financial constraint has stuck with me to this day. In that moment I told myself I would never find myself in that position ever again.

This experience molded the way I thought, felt, and acted with money for a very long time. It was a fiscal trauma that I unknowingly carried with me for years. Luckily for me, this incident produced a mostly positive money response; I started investing— squirreling away wads of cash in metaphorical underwear drawers in the form of real estate investments.

However, it wasn't all roses. Driven by the financial emotions surrounding my sister's accident, I felt as though I could never invest enough. I recall the down payment on one of my and Rosalie's real estate investments pushing our bank account balance below $1.70. Ironically, I was creating the same feeling of financial constraint by *over-investing.* It certainly wasn't logical. But emotions around money seldom are.

I didn't realize it at the time, but this experience was profoundly impactful. It wasn't until I started laying out all my patterns around money that I could address my attitude toward it, which is why I highly recommend you do the same.

I truly believe that in order to control how you behave with money, you first have to go into your past and figure out what's driving your behavior.

Your New Money Mantra

Everyone has the power within themselves to write their own money story. It's your responsibility to decide what you want that story to be.

Now you've examined your past experiences with money and recognized how they've shaped you, it's time to determine whether or not they are serving you. Are the stories you have been telling yourself about money helping you or holding you back? Is it time to let some of them go? What new powerful money stories should take their place?

I don't want to discount the money stories of your past because they have undoubtedly shaped you and are valid. But ultimately it is for you to decide whether to deal with those emotions or keep letting them dictate your life.

Instead of living through subconscious ideas about money that do not serve you, let's get intentional and create a new *money mantra*.

Remember, *we become what we think about, most of the time*. If our pre-existing money mindsets, along with the majority of those around us, are negative, we will simply gravitate towards money scarcity. Therefore, by re-writing your money beliefs and creating a new money mantra, you allow yourself to believe in positivity and abundance—which will let you grow into financial abundance.

My personal money mantra is *money magnifies my authentic impact*. I remind myself of this often and use it to guide me anytime I feel an emotional flare-up around money. It allows me to see how amazing a tool money can be when your money beliefs are aligned with your core values.

Essentially, because of my money mantra, I no longer feel bad or guilty about earning money because I know it allows me to have more of an impact. For example, I wouldn't have been able to co-launch *The Veterinary Project* podcast without having some extra money to fund it.

I recommend you create your own money mantra by doing what we talked about in this chapter. After letting go of money mindsets that do not serve you, analyzing why they exist, and creating a new money mantra, you'll officially have a fresh start with money. In the next chapter, we will be building on this with some new ways to think about money.

The $20 Bill

I now want you to refer back to the $20 bill you set out in the beginning of the chapter. What has it done the entire time it has been sitting there?

The answer is nothing. It has done absolutely nothing at all. It hasn't hurt you, corrupted you, made you more popular or affected your life in any way. Money doesn't think or feel or act. It only does *exactly* what you tell it to do.

But while money is neutral, you are not.

If money is affecting you in any way, it's because you are letting it affect you.

I hope this chapter has helped you become aware of those negative money mindsets that aren't serving you so you can dismantle them and replace them with more helpful ones. I truly believe that changing your money mindset to one of positivity and abundance is the key to improving a lot of the issues presented in this book and changing your life.

At the same time, while the $20 bill hasn't done anything to you while you've been reading, it also hasn't done anything *for* you. In the following chapter, we'll talk about the many ways money can work *for* you—not against you.

Chapter Thirteen

New Money Paradigms

ALLOW ME TO take a moment to congratulate you. The hard part is over!

Last chapter, we discussed how to analyze your money mindset and how to subsequently reframe money beliefs that aren't serving you—making room for a more positive, healthy relationship with money. This chapter is all about how you can supercharge how you create money, so that you can experience more abundance with less effort.

You may find that my philosophies below are the opposite of what you have learned conventionally about making money and building wealth. Many of these notions may counter popular opinion, but they are rooted in exciting new thinking about money, my years of researching those that have achieved financial success and following their lead, and the personal financial success I have found.

The purpose of this chapter is to help introduce you to fiscal lessons that greatly served me in my life as a vet—things I wish I had known earlier. I have no official financial credentials that qualify me to give you financial advice—but this is not financial advice!

Instead, these are simply lessons I have picked up from personal experience and by learning from others. That is why I will direct you to different resources throughout the text—think of this chapter as a jumping-off point!

First, you should know that these are advanced lessons. They build off the absolute foundational level of personal finances, which includes having (and sticking to) a budget, having proper insurance in place (critical illness, disability, life), and having an emergency fund. I am not saying that you should skip this foundational level. Go to a financial advisor for these things, and work on my tips next. My lessons are aggressive, but when properly executed they should never be reckless.

Second, my lessons are a playbook for achieving financial independence in 10 years instead of 35 or more. I am in no way saying that the traditional 35-year-plus plan as a veterinarian won't work. It probably will, but I have found that my methods just speed that up.

Now, before you read on, remember that if you want things in your life to be different, you'll have to do things in your life differently. And initially, that will fall outside of your comfort zone. With that in mind, here are my seven paradigms for financial freedom:

1. Diversification Is Dilution

2. Debt Is Good

3. Build Hopper Bins

4. Bet on Yourself

5. 2% Is Better than 10%

6. Retirement Is Dead

7. Multiple Streams of Income Are Mandatory

These seven paradigms have worked for me personally and changed my life—so well, in fact, that I have done and am actively still doing all of them. I'm not just offering you these things in theory: I walk this walk.

1. Diversification Is Dilution

If your net worth is less than $1 million, you should be intensely focused on one thing: whatever you want your primary financial instrument to be. It could be your career as a veterinary associate, specialist, or clinic owner. For me, it was real estate investing.

"Diversification is dilution" is a far cry from traditional financial sentiment in a world where diversification is often touted. But if your goal is to achieve complete financial independence in less than 10 years, you need to get moving and get focused—especially if you are a veterinarian that has missed out on years of earning an income and has student debt.

An analogy I like to use is getting an airplane off the ground. During takeoff, every single ounce of effort is placed on getting the plane in the air. It's the only thing that matters. There is no meal service or going to the washroom. Tray tables are up, seat belts are on, and the plane is going in one direction only. This is where the biggest amount of energy is required, just to get moving. Much less energy is consumed once you're in the air.

It's the same thing with earning money and building wealth when you're starting out. Figure out which direction you are heading and go all in. The first million is the hardest to earn and will require the most energy.

Starting out is also when you have the least to lose. Think about it, you can't lose money you don't have. If things don't go well on your first venture, you'll likely just find yourself back in the same situation you're already in. Furthermore, you can make bold moves with the benefit of a long-time horizon on your side. I am always looking for situations where there is an asymmetrical risk–reward ratio. Extreme focus early in your journey is one of those situations.

If you're going to be a veterinary specialist, become the best in your field. If you are going to own your own practice, invest in running it like a successful business. If you are going to take your paycheques and actively invest in real estate (or something else), get to know that investment industry inside and out.

If you spread yourself too thin with too much diversification, you will never be an expert at one thing. You will spend too much time and energy on too many things, which will prevent you from ever excelling at one of them.

Now, I'm sure you've heard that diversification is about minimizing risk, and it is. It's not that diversification is bad, but the time and place for diversification is not when you are starting out. *Concentration leads to growth*, and that is what is required to get your personal financial machine moving. It's like how a magnifying glass can produce enough energy to start a fire, but only when it's concentrating the sun's rays. Without the magnifying glass, the sun's rays are too spread out (or diversified) to start a fire. It is my belief that no one should remove their financial magnifying glass until their net worth is at about $1 million, but there is no definitive number.

Once your primary financial instrument is well established and producing significant results, only *then* should you consider diversifying.

I know this advice isn't traditional, but it reminds me of a saying from vet school: *The solution to pollution is dilution.* It makes sense that when you water down something that is polluted, it becomes more dilute (think of adding water to food coloring—the more water you add, the more the color will fade out until it eventually disappears entirely).

It works the same way with financial gains. If something is working well, why would you water it down? Shifting focus to anything else will just cause dilution and lower your overall result. In the financial sense, the saying could be modified to read: *Dilution is pollution, not the solution.*

2. Debt Is Good

There is a difference, of course, between good and bad debt.

Good debt is when you borrow money to invest in an asset. I would take this a step further to classify good debt as debt that will also service itself; that is, the debt will generate enough income to make its *own* payments. One final criteria of good debt is that the asset acquired is reasonably expected to appreciate in value over time.

I'm certainly not encouraging credit card and consumer debt here!

GOOD DEBT	BAD DEBT
☐ Used to acquire an asset ☐ Debt serviced/ paid by the asset acquired ☐ Asset acquired reasonably expected to appreciate in value over time	☐ Used to acquire a liability ☐ Debt needs to be serviced/paid by some other source of income (usually your paycheque) ☐ Liability acquired depreciates in value over time
Tier-one examples: *Vet clinic, an income-producing investment in real estate*	*Tier-one examples:* *Consumer goods on credit card*

One of the biggest financial benefits I've ever experienced from being a veterinarian is the ability to borrow money simply because I am a veterinarian with a stable, well-paying job. You must have near perfect financial discipline to take on large amounts of good investment debt, but doing so can be incredibly powerful if executed properly.

Almost all my debt came in the form of mortgages that were used to purchase investment real estate. The rent generated by these investments was more than enough to cover all my mortgage payments as well as other expenses. *This strategy alone has easily contributed more to my net worth than the cumulative total of all my veterinary paycheques.*

I understand it can be a little frightening to borrow money, so it's critical that we learn to differentiate between good and bad debt, and to see good debt as the powerful tool that it is. (For more on this, check out Episode 38 on *The Veterinary Project* podcast, titled, "Financial Literacy—What You Need to Know About Debt.")[46]

To illustrate, let's once again think of a scalpel blade—a sharp and potentially dangerous tool. You would never just start waving a scalpel blade around, making careless incisions, or put a scalpel blade in the hands of toddler—you understand that each incision with a scalpel blade should be deliberate and well thought out. In the hands of a knowledgeable and experienced veterinarian, a scalpel blade becomes a powerful tool that can heal and save lives. The exact same tool has the capacity to do both good and bad, but it all depends on how it's used. It's not an instrument to be feared, but it must be respected.

Good debt is the scalpel blade in a lifesaving surgical incision. It is a powerful instrument you can use to propel your personal finances forward. Good debt also moves time forward. Just think about how long it would take you to save up all the money you would need to buy or start your own veterinary clinic (likely many years). With good debt, you can accomplish this in months.

You've heard that it takes money to make money. It's true, but it doesn't need to be *your* money! The bank's money will do just fine...

3. **Build Hopper Bins**

On my family's farm, we had two kinds of grain bins. Some were flat on the bottom, so to get the grain out, we'd have to get inside and shovel it out—it was hard, exhausting work. The other type of bin had a funnel-shaped base, also known as a *hopper bin*. The grain could exit easily without much effort on our end.

One very hot summer day, I was working on building one of these flat-bottom bins. I remember how much sweat was pouring down my face when I turned to my dad and complained, "This is a lot of work, and it always will be." We both immediately realized that our time and effort would have been better spent building hopper bins.

It really is a no-brainer when you think about it. Why would I want to have to climb into the same bin, over and over again, to reap the same reward? Wouldn't I rather put a system in place that I can use repeatedly and effortlessly?

I ask these questions whenever I want to purchase something, whether it's a car or cooking services. I'm always looking for areas where I can put an asset in place that will pay for that item or service repeatedly, month after month, without me having to figuratively "climb back in the bin each time."

For instance, I've invested in various stocks that pay me dividends, which I use to cover the cost of my family's cooking service. The dividends are a hopper bin that will continue to pay for my family's meals without any time or effort on my part. The asset I have put in place pays for the items I purchase. This is a very important distinction as you'll note that earned income (such as a paycheque) *does not* purchase these items directly. The best use of my time, energy, and earned income is to continually focus on building hopper bin assets and let them purchase the things I enjoy in life.

Note the subtle but important distinction: Rosalie and I do not have help around the house because we are wealthy.

We are wealthy *because* we have help around the house. The assistance we receive frees up our time and energy to go out into the world and build more hopper bins!

Where can you add a hopper bin into your life? Well, if you want to enjoy Starbucks coffee, why not buy Starbucks stock and let its dividend pay for your beverages. Want to live mortgage free? Buy a house that has multiple suites, rent out the portions you aren't using, and live for free. A great place to start is to hire out or put systems in place for any task that costs less than your hourly wage. For example, if you can hire a house cleaner at $25 an hour and you earn $50+ an hour as a vet, why are you spending your time cleaning? You shouldn't be unless it's something you love and it brings you joy.

Never underestimate the power of putting one of these small systems in place. Every single one of them creates time in your life, truly your most valuable asset, and moves you one step closer to financial independence.

Another major benefit of putting hopper bins in place is that they produce recurring revenue—like virtually every other industry these days. Think of all the subscription-based services you might participate in such as Netflix or a cell phone plan. Even the veterinary industry is gravitating toward these models with subscription food delivery and in-clinic wellness plans for clients.

Can you guess my favorite recurring revenue stream of all? Collecting monthly rent!

4. Bet on Yourself

Every single person I have met who has achieved financial independence in a short (~10 years) period, at one point or another took a calculated risk and invested heavily in themselves.

They invested in something they were directly in control of and had influence over, like starting their own business. In such a case, the business' success came as a direct result of their efforts. They didn't hand the financial reins over to someone else and say, "Here, do it for me." They took charge, maintained control, and went all in with confidence in themselves.

At some point, you will need to make big, committed decisions in your life if you want to reach your financial goals. I'm warning you now, you will need to take a leap of faith and there will be an element of risk involved. Although the end result will be unknown at the start, investing in yourself is a calculated risk with rewards that are *worth it.*

During this period of your life, you will be severely out of balance by all traditional financial metrics. A disproportionately large amount of your net worth and debt liabilities will likely be tied up in one single pursuit. The good news is that the financial rewards that follow this relentless determination can be enormous and will change the course of your life.

You will *also* be severely out of kilter on the whole work/life balance scale. It is easy to get misled by social media and think that entrepreneurship and business ownership is all nice meals and beach vacations. Yes, those things can come, but typically after *years* of intense focus.

Of course, you don't have to follow a path that involves such a huge leap of faith and increased levels of risk. Veterinarians are fortunate because financial independence is achievable on a more traditional, 30-year timeline. But if you want to shorten that timeline, you will need to do things differently. If you are a veterinarian with the interest, desire, and commitment to pursuing veterinary clinic ownership, it could be one of the most rewarding financial endeavours of your life.

5. 2% Is Better than 10%

On my journey to financial independence, this was a mind-blowing concept.

When given the choice between a 2% and 10% return, which would you choose? Most people naturally gravitate toward the higher number, as I did. This is because we are conditioned to think only about the rate of return, and not about the *speed* of that return.

Enter the idea of *velocity of money*. Velocity of money refers to how quickly you can deploy your capital, have it generate a return, and then recover it so you can do it again. It's more of a continual cycle, rather than an annual number.

In an effort to explain this concept let's tie the term "currency" to the word "current," whereby the traditional model of personal finance wants us to "park" our money by putting our paycheque in a savings account or mutual fund. However, when considering the *velocity of money,* our "currency" is meant to flow, like a current. The more it can flow, the more you can generate.

Here's where it all comes together: Earning 2% every month would, in reality, be a better return than earning 10% every year.

Most people think of investing as taking a chunk of money, buying a mutual fund, and forgetting about it for 30 years. This is parking your money and it hasn't worked all that well for me, personally speaking.

Most of my financial success has come from cycling my money—allowing it to flow. In the real estate world, this looks like buying a property, fixing it up, renting it out, refinancing the property to recover all the money I put into it, and then doing it all over again! Even better, I continue to collect rent from this first property even though my money has moved on to the next property. In this way, the same initial chunk of capital I originally invested is used repeatedly to build multiple revenue streams, which continue to pay me long after the work has been done.

Kind of like building another hopper bin while the first one keeps working for you!

6. **Retirement Is Dead**

The concept of traditional retirement goes something like this: Work hard your entire life to save up a large pile of money. Use said large pile of money to live off when you decide to stop working. Hope to die before your money runs out.

Sounds fun.

Honestly, I despise the concept of traditional retirement. Having to constantly worry that you won't have enough saved in old age, trying your best to pace the money out, and then stress that you might live *too long* seems absurd to me.

I much prefer the thought of financial independence, where you can start living your best life much sooner. Once your passive income streams exceed your living expenses, you can choose to work or not. With financial independence, it doesn't matter how long you live because your monthly income exceeds your expenses. And if you continue to invest any excess you make, your financial quality of life *increasingly improves*—even into old age.

Age and working become irrelevant if you have financial independence. Imagine being 40 years old and choosing whether or not you want to work? You could still see some puppies and kittens if you wanted to, but you don't *have* to anymore. Isn't that freeing?

7. Multiple Streams of Income Are Mandatory

This may be a little bit confusing. On one hand, I'm telling you that diversification is dilution, but on the other, I'm telling you that you need to have multiple sources of income. Both are correct—they just come at opposite ends of the journey.

First, as I've said above, get one source of income solidly established, and only then add an additional one and continue to diversify.

Relying on just one source of income is the *riskiest* position you can be in. Having only a paycheque from your veterinary career means you are just one step away from having *zero* income. Even though we traditionally have very secure jobs, in my opinion, it is still an extremely high-risk position to be in. If you lose that source of income, you lose 100% of your earnings.

Just ask yourself, why do you double ligate?

Imagine being in the middle of the largest, most obese in-heat dog spay you have ever experienced. When it comes time to ligate the ovarian blood vessels, are you confident enough to just place one ligature? Sure, most of the time your one, well-placed ligature is sufficient, but then why do many people double ligate anyway?

For safety. Though it's unlikely that one of your ligatures will fail, the probability is still higher than zero. So, there is a chance that disaster can strike. Placing a second one helps us sleep well at night. The consequences of relying on just one ligature and having it fail are just too severe.

This is the same as relying on one single stream of income via a paycheque. Sure, most of the time it works, and you may even make it through your entire life never experiencing the pain of having it disappear. But the chances that it could someday, without warning, disappear are very real.

Therefore, it is essential that you:

1. **Protect your ability to earn income when you are starting out.** When we're just beginning as veterinarians, our ability to earn income is exceptionally valuable because we don't yet have the capital needed to pursue other investments. Protect that ability with proper insurance (like critical illness, disability, etc.).

2. **Secure multiple streams of income as soon as you can.** This can be just an offshoot of an existing stream of income or something totally new. For instance, a vet clinic could add in new services like ultrasound, dental, boarding, etc., new revenue streams that also diversifies the business. Alternatively, a vet clinic owner with a well-running business could invest in a completely unrelated, publicly traded dividend stock.

As you move closer to true financial independence, you will want to protect yourself with more and more streams of income—in other words, multiple investments, not just one. Now that your plane is in the air, it is way more important for it to *not* crash than it is for it to go fast.

How Do You Earn Money?

Robert Kiyosaki's Cashflow Quadrant illustrates an important concept.[47] He talks about four different quadrants, or ways, that you can earn money. The *E, S, B,* and the *I.*

Picture a cross in your mind. In the top left corner is the "E," an employee who trades time for money. This is the traditional, classic category most people fall into, from fast-food worker to associate veterinarian.

In the bottom left, there's an "S" for self-employed. The person could be a plumber or a certain type of veterinarian. They are more specialized and typically earn a little more than the employee. They may get to control their own hours, but that person is still trading time for money.

In the top right, you will find a "B," someone who owns or runs a business. In that model, the owner makes money on a process and a system that *should* be able to operate even when that person is absent. When "B" is done well, you aren't technically trading time for money, but most people don't do "B" well.

Many veterinarians find themselves in a trap where, although they technically own a business, it cannot operate without them being physically present. There aren't any systems, processes, or people in place to keep the business running without them. Therefore, even though they think they're in the "B" quadrant, they're really behaving like they're in the "S" quadrant. Although this can be quite lucrative, it still requires trading your time for money in some capacity.

The "I" in the bottom right stands for investor. As an investor, you exchange your money to earn more money. Your money heads out to work *for* you with the intention of growing. For the first time, you do not have to exchange your time for money!

These four quadrants are not all or nothing: you can exist in many of them at the same time—employee and investor, business owner and investor. The key concept here is to simply be aware of where your income is coming from. Income from the "E" and "S" quadrants are limited by time. Income from the "B" and "I" quadrants are typically unlimited.

The moment I was aware of this map, it became my life mission to derive more and more of my income from the right side of the quadrant. These efforts compound, and with enough time and effort, income from the right side of the quadrant can dwarf that from the left side. When this happens, you have complete control over your time.

For more takes on the Cashflow Quadrant, check out episode 47 of *The Veterinary Project* podcast called, "The Cashflow Quadrant: How Do You Make Your Money?"[48]

Real Estate

I've found that the best way I could lean into the "I" quadrant was through real estate. It has made a profound impact on my life, and I fully believe that real estate investing can completely change the financial future of anyone reading this book.

Don't worry, I'm not trying to convince you to become a real estate "junkie" like me, but I do believe there are some ways it benefits veterinarians specifically and can expedite your journey to financial freedom:

1. **House Hacking:** Everyone needs to live somewhere, so turn this from an expense to a revenue stream. This may be more applicable to students, but I believe that at any point in life you can find a property to live in and rent out portions of it you don't use to offset your cost of living. The goal should be to live for free, or ideally make money each month.

2. **Access to Credit/Capital:** Banks line up to give vets with a stable income "good debt" when it is secured against a real asset, such as real estate. Take it and use it to your advantage. **Bonus Pro-Tip:** Access as much as you can in the form of lines of credit long before you need them. You only pay interest if you actually use them, so it's fine for them to just sit there. And the best investment opportunities seldom give you advanced notice. Be prepared.

3. **Scalability:** My real estate ventures started as a side hustle, but then became a full-time thing. Either way, you can have one property or many.

4. **Inflation Protection:** Notice how your paycheque hasn't kept up with the value of your home? Real estate is a hard asset, whereas fiat currency, i.e. the money you are paid in, is not. Inflation erodes fiat currency, whereas real estate assets protect your wealth from inflation. You must own *real* assets!

5. **Hard Asset Growth:** Due to inflation, hard assets, like real estate, tend to grow more than money on its own does. In fact, the growing divide between rich and poor seems to come down to owning hard assets—even if you make $100K a year. Money alone just doesn't go as far as it used to.

I view real estate investing as a three-course meal, with an appetizer, a main course, and a dessert.

The appetizer is the cashflow that your investment property will pay you each and every month. Cashflow is simply all the revenue that a property generates (mostly in the form of rent) minus all expenses. Some of these expenses may be mortgage payments, property tax, insurance, property management, maintenance, bank fees, and more. A real estate investment *must* be cashflow positive. If it is not, I walk away.

The main course, which is your mortgage paydown, is the meat and potatoes of your investment. Every month the rent that you collect will pay your mortgage payment. And every month, as your mortgage balance goes down, your equity in your asset will increase. How nice is that? It's like a forced savings plan, except you aren't the one that has to put the money in the piggy bank!

Of course, no one invests in real estate thinking there will be no appreciation. This brings us to dessert, the final part of our meal.

Appreciation is the cherry on top in real estate investing! These are the fantastical stories of people buying a house that triples in value in a few short years.

This is certainly possible in real estate, but it is not guaranteed, so I always caution veterinarians that consult with me about real estate investing not to expect or rely on their asset going up in value annually.

This also happens to be why appreciation is the dessert of real estate investing. It comes last and should never be relied on to make or break your meal!

❧

Real estate has completely changed my view on "retirement" and the trajectory of my life. When I think back to sitting at that red light on the way to my first day of work, I remember feeling completely dejected that I had entered the phase of my life that felt like a grind. *Do this for the next 35 years and then hopefully you'll be able to retire.*

Diving into real estate allowed me to flip this notion on its head. Thirty-five years became 10. My nine-to-five became any location, anytime. Limited income became unlimited.

If you want to learn more about real estate or connect on the subject, please feel free to reach out through my website: www.michaelbugg.com.

For all Veterinarians

People always ask me about my daily schedule and what my life is like. To this day, I still answer in the same way—with the kind of bewilderment that a child experiences on Christmas morning. "I can't believe people get to live this way!"

Of course, this doesn't mean my family and I are flying all over the world to exotic locales with private jets and yachts. It's quite the opposite, in fact. We aren't super rich and we actually lead a relatively simple life. But we do have systems in place that have helped us reach a baseline level of financial freedom. We are off the hamster wheel that comes with exchanging time for paycheques and will continue to expand on that. So, although we may not be rich, I do consider us wealthy.

One of my hopes with this book is to change the way veterinarians think about how they earn money. I believe that tailoring our income is the most holistic way to tackle the problems we see in our profession. I know this first-hand—gaining financial freedom had a huge impact on my quality of life and happiness within the veterinarian profession.

For example, one of the best ways to combat the burnout and overwhelm in veterinary medicine is to work less, but how can veterinarians do that? By having multiple streams of income in place outside of just collecting a regular paycheque.

Imagine being able to work only three days a week as a vet! Suddenly, the dial is turned down on many of the challenges we have previously discussed here.

There is an obvious and very dangerous trap in *needing* to trade time for money. Time is our most limited and non-renewable resource. Once you spend it, that time is gone forever. You will never get it back. I am not saying this because I believe veterinarians should never practice. I just see the possibility of veterinarians being able to do what they love! For many that will continue to mean that they practice—but on *their* schedule.

Wealth can be seen in terms of having a big house or a nice car, but that's not the case for me. Being able to sit down in the mornings with Rosalie, Riley, and Ethan, no matter the day of the week, and have a cup of coffee is wealth to me. No one else can see that, but it matters to me. Too often we get caught up in what the material possessions of financial freedom might look like. However, I've found that what most people really want is time freedom. The ability to do what they want, whenever they want.

I hope this chapter has shown you the many ways you can do that.

Remember, the $20 from last chapter will only do exactly what you tell it to do. So the real question now is: What are you going to let it do for you?

Chapter Fourteen

The ~~Red~~ Green Light

O**N MY LAST** day as a practicing veterinarian, I came home to a huge hug from Rosalie and a gift. At that point, I had decided to take the leap into real estate investing full time and explore new ways to be a part of the veterinary community.

She gave me the perfect gift that evening—a blazer with a pair of shoes for a real estate conference I had the next day, and a bottle of champagne. Inside the shoebox was a quote that read, "Do the future and never step back."

Rosalie didn't know that quote was printed on the box, but to me, it felt a bit like fate.

I kept that shoe box, and still have it to this day.

At the time, I didn't realize how much my life was going to evolve in the coming years, but I can say with full confidence that I'm glad I took that leap into the unknown.

Not everyone has to pivot in their career so dramatically like I did, but we should all look to foster the best version of our life *today* and into the future. Whatever that means for you could be very different compared to what it means for me.

And it all starts with a "step" forward.

Take Back Control

Being a veterinarian is a double-edged sword.

I believe the work we do is incredibly important. When you consider the special bonds created between humans and animals, it's evident that we are in a great position to impact humanity in a positive way. We are also in a great position to impact *the world* in a positive way, if you think about how significant animals are to ecosystems and the environment, and the link between human and animal health.

But all of this comes at a cost. Oftentimes, we sacrifice our well-being, time, and joy for the demands of others.

My hope is that this book has helped identify the many issues veterinarians deal with and has given you the resources you need to navigate them.

The thoughts and solutions written in these pages have changed my life. Perhaps they will do the same for you.

But that change won't start until you're an active driver in the journey that is your life. You've taken a great first step by stepping into your curiosity and reading this book. I hope it has caused some moments of pause and reflection for you, and I commend you for embracing them.

However, the work does not end here—in fact, you're just getting started. I encourage you to continue intentionally tailoring your life by implementing the strategies you've read here that work for you, exploring ways to design your life and finances, and by further educating yourself with great resources. One of the places you may want to continue the conversation is through *The Veterinary Project* podcast where Jonathan and I dive deeper into some of the topics discussed in this book and hear from other leaders in the veterinary profession.[49]

Remember, your happiness is within your control. Take action and seize it.

The Red Light

My wish is for everyone reading this book to have the most joyfully fulfilling career and life possible. In order for this to happen, every aspect of your life should align with your veterinary vision. And when it does, everything comes together with incredible synergy.

At times it may seem far away, but I'm telling you right now that *it is possible.* I know this first-hand.

Looking back, roughly 14 years after stopping at that red light on my way to the clinic for the first time, there is simply no way I could have predicted that this is where I'd be today. I don't own a veterinary clinic. I own more houses than cows (and I love cows). And I've journeyed to miserable and back.

The life I have today is exactly *nothing* like what I expected it to be on my veterinary graduation day. Hell, most of the things we've talked about in this book weren't even on my radar or in my vocabulary at that point.

I still think about that day, staring straight ahead into that red light. It seems so obvious now—but I just couldn't see it at the time. If I had just looked right or left, I would have been met with a green light. This can be your veterinary career—and your life.

It's about this time that one of the co-hosts of *The Veterinary Project* podcast chimes in with, "As always, the final word goes to you. What message do you want to leave for the veterinary community?"

And with that, I leave you with this:

The green lights are everywhere. You just have to look for them.

Acknowledgments

To Rosalie. This book is far more than just words written on paper. It is the capturing of the stories and experiences lived over the past decade plus. And no one has been more intimately involved in that journey than you. Thank you for being by my side through all the ups and downs and believing in me even when I didn't believe in myself. Writing this book was really a walk down memory lane and I'm so fortunate to have had your love and support through it all. There is no doubt in my mind that, without you, this book wouldn't exist, and I would be in a very different place. I'm excited for the future as we continue to add chapters! Just as you have done for me, I'll be there whenever you get peed on!

To Mom and Dad. Thank you for all your love and support. I know I was pretty much an angel growing up so raising me really wasn't all that hard, but thanks for all the patience and life lessons along the way. I'm thankful, too, for your financial foresight and support that allowed me to graduate from vet school with zero student debt and sound real estate investment, which allowed me to live rent free all through university. This, among many things, will never be forgotten.

To Tom. No one has taught me more about the world of veterinary medicine than you. I will be forever grateful to have had such an amazing mentor in my life from such an early age. The veterinary profession is lucky to have you and I'm honored to call you a friend.

To my early real estate supporters: Mom, Dad, Jamie, Michelle, Larry, and Audrey. Thank you for believing in Rosalie and me way back when all of this was just an idea. It hasn't all been smooth sailing but you have no idea how much your trust means to me.

To Julie Broad and the team at Book Launchers. Without you this book would still be unwritten. Thanks for holding my hand and walking me through it. Special shout out to Kate for all the hours spent on Zoom listening to my stories and ideas over and over.

To ~~Jonny~~ Jonathan. It's been a blast tackling *The Veterinary Project* podcast together! I've always been fascinated and inspired by your career and your ability to do your own thing. Nice moves, buddy!

Endnotes

1   For more on *The Veterinary Project* podcast, visit: https://linktr.ee/theveterinaryproject.

2   Chelsey L. Holden, "Characteristics of Veterinary Students: Perfectionism, Personality Factors, and Resilience," *Journey of Veterinary Medical Education* 47, no. 4 (May 15, 2020): 488–96, https://doi.org/10.3138/jvme.0918-111r.

3   Ibid.

4   Arlin Cuncic, "What Is Imposter Syndrome?" Verywell Mind, November 23, 2021, https://www.verywellmind.com/imposter-syndrome-and-social-anxiety-disorder-4156469.

5   Lori R. Kogan, Regina Schoenfeld-Tacher, Peter Hellyer, Emma K. Grigg, and Emily Kramer, "Veterinarians and impostor syndrome: an exploratory study," *VetRecord* 187, no. 7 (22 June, 2020): 271, https://doi.org/10.1136/vr.105914.

6   Dan Sullivan with Dr. Benjamin Hardy, *The Gap and the Gain: The High-Achievers' Guide to Happiness, Confidence, and Success* (Carlsbad, CA: Hay House Business, 2021).

7   Ibid.

8   "Veterinary Medicine is a Service Industry," *The Veterinary Project* podcast, July 28, 2020, 44 mins.

9   S. D. Buffington, *The Law of Abundance* (Torrance, CA: QuinStar Publishing, 2009).

10   David Schwartz, *The Magic of Thinking Big* (New York: Touchstone, 2015), 234.

11   "Travel, Debt and Business Opportunities with Dr. Dan Katz, D.V.M.," *The Veterinary Project* podcast, August 18, 2020, 43 mins.

12   Hal Elrod, *The Miracle Morning: The Not-So-Obvious Secret Guaranteed to Transform Your Life before 8AM* (n.p.: Hal Elrod International, Incorporated, 2012).

13   Ibid.

14   Eva M. Krockow, "How Many Decisions Do We Make Each Day?" *Psychology Today*, September 27, 2018, https://www.psychologytoday.com/us/blog/stretching-theory/201809/how-many-decisions-do-we-make-each-day.

15   For more on Dr. Devin Nobert's story, listen to part one and part two of our episode, "Overcoming Obstacles and Strength-Based Vulnerability with Dr. Devin Nobert," *The Veterinary Project* podcast, October 14, 2020, 47 mins.

16   Brennen A. McKenzie, "Veterinary clinical decision-making: cognitive biases, external constraints, and strategies for improvement," *Journal of the American Veterinary Medical Association* 224, no. 3 (February 1, 2014): 271–2, https://doi.org/10.2460/javma.244.3.271.

17   Tania Singer and Olga M. Klimecki, "Empathy and compassion," *Current Biology* 24, no. 18 (September 22, 2014): R875–8, https://www.doi.org/10.1016/j.cub.2014.06.054.

18   Trisha Dowling, "Compassion does not fatigue!" *The Canadian Veterinary Journal* 59, no. 7 (July 2018): 749–50, https://www.ncbi.nlm.nih.gov/pmc/articles/PMC6005077/.

19   Ibid.

20   Lisa Moses, Monica J. Malowney, and Jon Wesley Boyd, "Ethical conflict and moral distress in veterinary practice: A survey of North American veterinarians," *Journal of Veterinary Internal Medicine* 32, no. 6 (October 15, 2018): 2115–22, https://doi.org/10.1111/jvim.15315.

21   Ibid.

22   "The Demartini Value Determination Process," Demartini, accessed May 9, 2022, https://drdemartini.com/values/.

23   "Getting People Right with Veteran Coach Trevor Throness," *The Veterinary Project* podcast, June 9, 2021, 44 mins.

24   Brian Tracy, *Change Your Thinking, Change Your Life: How to Unlock Your Full Potential for Success and Achievement* (Hoboken, NJ: Wiley, 2011), xiv.

25   Goalcast, "How to Change the Way You See Yourself | Rock Thomas | Goalcast," YouTube video, February 12, 2018, https://www.youtube.com/watch?v=1IH-0digwjds.

26   Emma Young, "Lifting the lid on the unconscious," *New Scientist*, July 25, 2018, https://www.newscientist.com/article/mg23931880-400-lifting-the-lid-on-the-unconscious/.

27   James Clear, *Atomic Habits* (New York NY: Random House Business, 2018).

28   Kevin Trudeau, *Your Wish is Your Command*, audio CD (New York: Global Information Network, 2009).

29   Bronnie Ware, *The Top Five Regrets of the Dying: A Life Transformed by the Dearly Departing* (Carlsbad, CA: Hay House, 2010), 37.

30   Random addition to how I unlocked my runner identity: It didn't fully imbed until one day while scrolling Instagram. I was on a running page where I saw a picture of a fit dad out for a run with his kids in a stroller. I was able to point to it and say, "That!" Suddenly I could picture what I wanted, my desire to become that increased, and I committed to *being* that version of myself.

31   Bill Taylor, "What Breaking the 4-minute Mile Taught us About the Limits of Conventional Thinking," *Harvard Business Review*, March 9, 2018, https://hbr.org/2018/03/what-breaking-the-4-minute-mile-taught-us-about-the-limits-of-conventional-thinking.

32   Proctor Gallagher Institute, "The Vacuum Law of Prosperity | Bob Proctor," YouTube video, March 5, 2021, https://www.youtube.com/watch?v=48qDpQU_fbY.

33   Dr. Robyne Hanley-Dafoe, "Everyday Resiliency," June 2020, https://robyne-hd.ca/wp-content/uploads/2020/07/RobyneHD_EverydayResiliency_Jan2020.pdf.

34   Hanley-Dafoe, "Everyday Resiliency," 2.